NONPROFIT
TRANSFORMED

Compassion Fatigue – Self-Care – Resilience

CATHY PHELPS, MA, LCSW

ISBN 978-0-9962054-4-3

McIntire
• PUBLISHING SERVICES •
www.mcintirepublishing.com

About the Author

Cathy Phelps, MA, LCSW, is the executive director for The Center for Trauma & Resilience (formerly The Denver Center for Crime Victims) in Denver, Colorado. CTR is a 29-year-old nonprofit agency recognized as a national model for providing culturally and linguistically responsive services, health promotion, and crime prevention education. The agency offers a 24-hour hotline, crisis counseling, advocacy and case management, a trauma-sensitive yoga program, and crime prevention education. It also offers specialized programs for children and their families and for seniors, and legal immigration services through Mi Gente–VAWA Legal Solutions.

The agency has a number of earned-income ventures including Health Enabling for the Listening Professional (HELP), which provides vicarious trauma training and resiliency-building strategies for the human service professional, and the agency's jewel—The Translation & Interpreting Center, which offers services in more than 40 languages and dialects. The Center for Trauma & Resilience was featured on Oprah Winfrey's "Pay It Forward" program and in *The Chronicle of Philanthropy*'s "Employee-Wellness Programs Pay Off in Productivity and Morale." Cathy was recognized by The Denver Foundation in "Inside Inclusiveness: Race, Ethnicity and Nonprofit Organizations."

With Cathy at the helm, the agency was a proud recipient of a Martin Luther King, Jr., Business Social Responsibility Award for excellence in programs, agency structure, and stability and was voted "One of the Best Companies for Working Families" by *Colorado Parent* magazine. In 2015, the agency was chosen by *The NonProfit Times* (NPT) as a 2015 NPT Best Nonprofit to Work For, ranking as one of the top five nonprofits in the United States.

Concurrent with her position at The Center for Trauma & Resilience, Cathy serves as part-time faculty for Metropolitan State University and the University of Colorado at Denver.

Cathy presented and published a paper entitled *The Legacy Continues: Rape Culture and African American Women* for the National Symposium on Non-Stranger Sexual Assault. She authored *Sexually Transmitted Diseases and HIV/AIDS in Adult Victim/Survivors of Sexual Assault in Colorado* and is a co-author of *Safe, Strong and Free: A Leader's Guide to Child Assault Prevention.*

Cathy earned her master of arts in medical anthropology from the University of Colorado Denver and a master of social work (MSW) from the University of Denver.

Contents

Appendix A: The Center for Trauma & Resilience Forms

Appendix A-1: New Employee Checklist

Appendix A-2: Oath of Confidentiality

Appendix A-3: Presentation of Self-Assessment Guidelines

Appendix A-4: Safety Policy Statement

Appendix A-5: Conflict Resolution Guidelines and Acknowledgment
    of Receipt

Appendix A-6: Vacation Leave and Donor Form

Appendix A-7: Case Presentation Outline

Appendix A-8: Quality Assurance Guidelines

Appendix A-9: Suggestions for Choosing a Therapist

Appendix B: Sample Self-Care Forms

Appendix B-1: Developing Your Self-Care Plan

Appendix B-2: Self-Care Progress Report

Appendix B-3: Self-Care Goal Examples

Appendix B-4: Kathi Fanning's 2012 — 100 "Things-To-Do" List

Appendix C: Other Forms

Appendix C-1: Staff Mission Statement

Appendix C-2: Inclusiveness Philosophy

Appendix C-3: Inclusiveness Activity Examples

Appendix C-4: BLEAP (Bettering the Lives of Employees and
    Agency Programs)

Appendix C-5: Potluck Sign-up

Foreword

Organizations have four kinds of resources: people, money, information, and time. The balance among these resources defines the agency. Of these, people are the most important, for without the right people with the right skills, no amount of funding can sustain the mission. And information will not flow. And time will always be too short. Rightly so, this book focuses on people and how to help all workers develop into the best they can be, while simultaneously helping the agency be as effective as it can.

Packed inside this book is a treasure trove of guidance on how to direct and manage a workforce of helping professionals. Providing services to people in need means that workers encounter emotionally intense dramas on a daily basis. How can staff stay fresh? How can they be caring, day after day, client after client? How can they listen with compassion when they have heard similar anguishing stories too many times? What keeps them coming back tomorrow to do the same work they did today? These are questions that confront executive directors and boards of directors across the nation.

This gem of a book discusses the importance of a self-care plan program and details how to implement it in an agency in a step-by-step fashion. It is an instrument designed to help staff perform emotionally intense work day after day, and still come back the next with compassion and empathy. It takes energy to hear hard stories, and it takes special skills to connect with clients and give meaningful responses. This is emotional labor, and it requires that staff manage their own emotions while responding to the emotional state of the other, whether patient, client, or victim.

Emotional labor is analogous to cognitive and manual labor. While emotional labor requires the management of one's own emotional state as well as sensitivity to that of the client, cognitive labor requires workers to use factual knowledge such as that presented in textbooks. The latter includes the ability to anticipate and plan and to translate similarities from one situation to another. Similarly, manual labor relies on physical skills. But it is emotional labor that is the least visible, least understood, but most potentially endangering to workers in human services agencies.

Workers' emotional intelligence is called upon as they perform emotional labor. This involves emotional self-awareness, awareness of the other person's emotional state, and the ability to regulate one's own emotions. Self-regulation refers to the worker's ability to suppress feelings of fear, or sadness, or disgust, while exhibiting compassion and empathy. Staff members vary in their level of proficiency with each of these, just as they vary in cognitive or physical skills.

Faced with panicked or traumatized victims, caseworkers and call-takers must size up a situation based on speech and body language and immediately determine how to respond. They have to establish trust and elicit cooperation, and they have to remain calm and composed while learning of the horrific circumstances that brought the client for services. Their response must be on the mark, for there are no "do-overs." Every word spoken matters. Workers who cannot manage their own emotional state as well as that of their clients fail to do their job, just as surely as does the physical laborer who cannot lift or carry weight. It is hard work and can scar the psyche.

Over the long-term, working in emotionally intense jobs is rich and meaningful because workers know they are making a difference in others' lives. In fact, they chose their careers for this reason. But the work can also have negative consequences and result in burnout, which has a corrosive effect, dampening reactivity and reducing emotional responsiveness to positive events both on the job and in workers' personal lives.

The emotive component that comes with working with people in distress is a huge part of each worker's routine performance. It is the "juice" that gives meaning to their work and motivates them. They know they are making a difference in others' lives. But it also has a downside, because it is emotionally demanding. The probability of burnout is high, and this is why the self-care plan is so important. As described so well in this book, it can be applied in a variety of settings and is a daily reminder to staff that they not only have obligations to others, but they also have obligations to themselves. To help someone else, they must be personally healthy. The unique strength of the self-care plan is that it develops a person's self-awareness at the same time that it develops coping mechanisms and opens workers to a larger sense of their own capabilities.

As an instrument, the plan insists that workers integrate their personal lives and differentiate their personal growth from that of the clients with whom they work. Achieving self-goals in the interest of being personally healthy frees the worker to be compassionate while not getting sucked into an emotional vortex. I commend this book to you and look forward to a time when self-care plans are used so widely that they are taken for granted as a part of each helping professional's dossier.

Mary E. Guy, PhD
Professor of Public Administration
University of Colorado at Denver
School of Public Affairs

Introduction

Twelve years ago I designed and implemented this self-care program for agency staff members who employ emotional labor in their work with trauma survivors. In addition, I have piloted and put into practice complementary management principles that I credit for my personal and organizational success.

The research literature on compassion fatigue and vicarious trauma is conclusive—those professionals who consistently work with traumatized individuals absorb their clients' distress, compromising their own health and clinical efficacy. The literature suggests that agency culture and environment can exacerbate these issues and become an occupational hazard for employees. Conversely, if organizations acknowledge the risks, prepare staff for that potential, and construct supportive infrastructures, they can assist employees in the prevention or mitigation of vicarious trauma.

Our program has been recognized, evaluated, and celebrated as a best practice for professionals working with traumatized individuals. Our most recent honor was having our agency chosen by *The NonProfit Times* (NPT) as a 2015 NPT Best Nonprofit to Work For, ranking our agency as one of the top five nonprofits in which to work in the United States.

Through this book I offer encouragement for other agencies to integrate self-care and institutional wellness policies. My dream is to build a team of successors who will continue to evolve and integrate this most important and vital work so they too can reap the emotional and professional rewards for both themselves and by extension, their clients and their community.

Acknowledgments

There are many hands and hearts that contributed to the realization of this book in a variety of ways—literally, emotionally, and figuratively. In alphabetical order they are: Carroll Watkins Ali (Sadikia), TaShia Asanti, Elizabeth Avendano, Rochelle Barber, Gail S. Bernstein, Lisa Calderon, Carmen Carrillo, Magda Y. Chia, Nan Clydesdale, Almeta Corbin, Joseph Do, Senakhu Donald, Kathi Fanning, Andrea Kawulok, Pamela Liverpool, Linda Mizell, Joan Njagu, Christina Hong Paguyo, Judith Schwartz, Lynn Smith, Amy Ulrich, Lisa Wolff, and the members of SASS (Sister Activists, Students and Scholars, Friday night writing group).

I am grateful and appreciative to Jean Trombley, the founding executive director. And for Arthur McDermott, my first board president and champion, who hired me and believed in me from the beginning. Steve Siegel and Irene Blatnik and the Denver VALE board members, who set a high bar and supported our stretch to meet it. As well as a plethora of administrators, funders, and donors, including (posthumously) Rob Gallup, and The Denver Foundation and The Rose Foundation.

I acknowledge The Center for Trauma & Resilience employees who secured our place as one of *The NonProfit Times* (TOP 5) Best Nonprofits to Work For—2015. They are: Ashley Brown, Kathi Fanning, Mario Flowers, Georgina Gutierrez, Fatima Garcia, Daysse Maryan Gomez, Carina Banuelos Harrison, Divenia Johnson, Daiga Keller, Pamela Liverpool, Rachel Muhito, Enid Nieves, Claudia Ortega, Janice Rhyne, Amy Ulrich, and Sharon Wood. And, Kent Webb, who has served as the clinical consultant for the organization for 28 years!

Thank you to my personal trainer, Stacia Miller, and my massage therapists, Desiree Sandoval and Victoria Sweet—my wellness team. Applause to my editorial magician Anne Serrano and to Rebecca Arno, who introduced us. And gratitude goes to a host of board members and employees with whom I worked over the past 12 years.

Finally, I want to pay homage to members of my ancestral family, my aunts Helen Smith Payne and Lois Smith Lewis, and my grandmother Macy Smith and grandfather Burrell Smith, who would not let me rest without completing this task.

CHAPTER 1

Taking Care of Business Means Taking Care of Our People

I began writing this book after receiving dozens of requests to share my agency's program on self-care. Some thought it was a bit of a novelty and were intrigued by my "social work" applications. Several colleagues desired a quick fix to whatever was ailing their particular nonprofit, but were resistant to "reworking the whole organization." However, far too many leaders continue to dismiss the idea, looking for forces (for example, funders) outside of their agency to blame for their agency's lack of success.

Positioning an agency as a group of "saints and servant leaders" works for a while, but the turmoil, turnover, and stagnation take their toll, and soon the agency either treads water, attempts a dramatic program or mission change (having neither the energy nor expertise to implement them), or dissolves.

WHO WE ARE AND WHERE WE WORK

For individuals working in an agency that deals with trauma, thinking of ourselves as "saints" or "servant leaders" is familiar. Our ego finds comfort in being "one of the good guys." We are the folks downstream from the flood—waiting for the next wave of crime, trauma, disaster, or mass tragedy to strike—and we busy ourselves in recovery efforts. We spring into action, believing that our piecemeal approach will be meaningful. Once one event is over, we move quickly toward the next one, leaving worn-out workers in its wake.

We are less likely to turn our attention inward, and invest in or ponder an upstream approach. We want it to be easier. We believe we have the answers (if we just had enough money!). We continue building homogenized collaborations and resource networks, ignoring environmental and community health conditions of our whole community. By applying a one-size-fits-all approach we disregard elements such as the poverty, racism, and educational and health inequities that overwhelm our clients and staff. We are busy rescuing people.

During the past 20 years, human services, and specifically services for crime victims, witnessed a rapidly changing and challenging terrain. Along with familiar criminal acts such as theft, aggravated assault, domestic and sexual violence, and homicide, we are also learning how to assist with home invasions (that is, when the primary victim is at home), identity theft, crimes committed using electronic tools (for example, cyber stalking, sexting), and horrific shootings in schools, movie theaters, and other places where we least expect gun violence. Human services staff have had to learn to negotiate civil remedies for immigrants who are victims of trafficking and other forms of interpersonal violence.

We are experimenting with new interventions and practices to grapple with the effects of trauma on our clients and in our communities. In addition, we have come to recognize the negative effects our work has on our staff members and ourselves—something to which we have not previously paid great attention.

In general, nonprofits lag behind the corporate and business sectors, which have begun to recognize that chronic stress (traumatic or not) is endemic in the workplace. A Career Builder study reported that, at any given time, 78 percent of workers stated that they worked in a high-pressure environment and felt burned out at their job. (Grasz, 2008).

Our environment is no exception. We work day in and day out with traumatized individuals in a setting where compassion and empathy are necessary attributes and skills. The daily challenges render workers vulnerable for burnout, compassion fatigue, and/or vicarious trauma.

The willingness of nonprofit executives to acknowledge that these negative effects exist and actively take steps to nurture and sustain staff in a health-promoting environment will ultimately prove to be as valuable as an endowment for their nonprofit. In her essay "Philanthropy's Greatest Asset" published in *Foundation News & Commentary,* the CEO of Grantmakers for Effective Organizations, Kathleen P. Enright, says, "The nonprofit sector is rapidly learning something that corporate America seems to already know." (Enright, 2006, p. 44). Committed people are the heart of every innovation and every bit of program the nonprofit sector makes, yet we consistently and habitually neglect this most valuable asset. She echoes James Carville: "It's the people, stupid." (Enright, 2006, p. 44). We must take care of our people.

Nonprofit executives need a variety of skill sets that include setting the strategic vision, fundraising, "friend-raising," attending to human resources, and responding to a board of directors. Executives focus on remaining afloat in a sea of need and competition for dollars. Those executives, reluctant or unable to provide a hands-on approach, delegate someone else to supervise, counsel, recognize, and evaluate the performance of supervisees. I prefer the hands-on method.

In their article "Organizational Prevention of Vicarious Trauma" published in *Families in Society: The Journal of Contemporary Human Services,* Bell, Kulkarni, and Dalton acknowledged that the difficult work of providing services to individuals, families, and communities often takes an emotional and psychological toll on workers. And, they state, the organization along with the workers may develop *trauma-based behaviors,* also known as "traumatized organizational culture." (Bell, Kulkarni, & Dalton, 2003). However, the literature spotlight has primarily centered on encouraging management to pay attention to increasing worker awareness and suggesting interventions for *individuals.* Little attention is given to the organization's infrastructure, administration, management practices, community demographics, and the role these aspects may contribute to the issue of vicarious trauma. In the article, the authors outline recommendations for settings where there are high levels of traumatized clients and state that "organizations have both a practical and ethical responsibility to address this risk." (Bell, Kulkarni, & Dalton, 2003, p. 465).

Since the inception of our self-care program at The Center for Trauma & Resilience, I have learned that the success of any individualized self-care plan is, in large part, based on its integration into the agency infrastructure. Self-care is part of every staff job description, weighted equally with all position objectives and part of every annual performance review.

The individualized self-care plan is only one component of my proposed nonprofit wellness paradigm. It is the individualized tool that may assist employees (and volunteers or interns) to cope with the complex task of dealing with secondary and vicarious trauma while working with intimate partner violence and other types of crime.

Any individualized self-care plan will falter if it is not supported by management principles and practices. The practice of self-care must be viewed as part of the fabric or heart of the agency. We have learned (haven't we?) that an additive or tokenism approach is not successful or sustainable for any true quest to develop an ethnically, culturally diverse, and inclusive workplace. In my experience more is needed in order to sustain a self-care practice. If isolated from other wellness practices, the idea of self-care is just that, only an idea.

I have learned through many years of experience leading an agency that there is no right path or single best way. Any effort to design and incorporate an agency wellness plan should be customized to your environment. The plan should be visionary, flexible, and inform decision-making. At its core, a self-care tool is inclusive, participatory, and will likely sustain itself if grounded in a health-promoting environment.

A UNIQUE NONPROFIT

Please permit me to share a little bit about my agency. In the late fall of 2001, I accepted the position of executive director for The Center for Trauma & Resilience (CTR). We were inaugurated in 1987 and are an award-winning nonprofit located in Denver, Colorado. Similar to many traditional victim assistance agencies, CTR provided 24-hour hotline crisis counseling and referrals from its onset. The hotline was primarily staffed by community volunteers and one or two staff members. We offered little in the manner of case management or health promotion. Our initial, respectable mission was to be an agency *"that provides services to crime victims and crime prevention education."* We held membership in a network of 30 victim services organizations, all of which agreed that "diversity" was a "good idea," and we agreed to realize it in our programs at The Center for Trauma & Resilience.

In 2013, after seven years of institutionalizing inclusiveness and diversity, offering individualized self-care plans, and encouraging health promotion for our staff members and clients, our mission expanded. Our mission now reads that we are an agency that *"provides culturally and linguistically responsive programs, health promotion, and crime prevention education."* We have been recognized as a national model that is unique in its ability to provide this depth and breadth of services to a broad range of crime victims, without cost, to all of the clients we serve.

Our program includes specialists for children and their families. We offer services for the elderly and people with disabilities. We host workshops for grandparents/kinship circles for those who are raising children who have been abused or abandoned, or for whom the primary parent has been the victim of a homicide or suicide. Mi Gente–VAWA Legal Solutions is a legal immigration service that assists physically and sexually abused immigrants from more than 25 countries.

The agency bar is high. The Center for Trauma & Resilience serves 1,500 people a year for whom we advocate, counsel, support, and broker services. We assist any affected party: the primary victim, co-victims, or their families and friends. We also provide services to witnesses or others affected by the crime. Annually, staff members give out information and referrals to more than 5,000 hotline callers.

All clients receive client-centered, trauma-informed assessments, case management, advocacy, and, upon request, accompaniment to other service providers. Staff members conduct approximately 1,000 counseling sessions both on-site and in clients' homes, as well as psycho-educational and trauma-informed groups for children and adults. We have the incredible good fortune to be able to provide emergency financial assistance in the form of food certificates, bus passes, and gift cards; to replace identification documents; and to facilitate home repairs, rent/relocation, medical prescriptions, and crime scene cleanup, among other services. After we complete our work with a client, we evaluate our services through pre- and post-group evaluation surveys and conduct monthly internal quality assurance reviews and client satisfaction surveys.

Administratively, counselors participate in weekly case management, clinical supervision, and educational in-services. We offer 40-hour advocate/internship training and internship placements for undergraduate and graduate students. Upon completion of attending our speakers' bureau, staff members perform more than 100 community presentations annually. Staff personnel organize quarterly social justice/diversity/ inclusiveness forums and manage a resource directory with more than 600 therapist and community vendors.

We design and host two major fundraising events each year, "That Jazz Thing" and "Denver Men with Heart," that augment other standard nonprofit development activities, which include grant writing, mid- and end-year donor appeals, and responses to ideas from donors and board members. Our agency jewel, The Translation & Interpreting Center, was our first earned-income venture and continues to provide language support (without cost to crime victims) in more than 40 languages and dialects.

In 2008, we launched our second earned-income social enterprise, entitled Health Enabling for Listening Professionals (HELP), a full-day experiential workshop to address secondary trauma for those who bear witness to others' pain or trauma. The daylong workshop offers trauma education during the morning and dedicates the afternoon to stress management and resilience-building activities, such as meditation, yoga, aromatherapy, crafting a journal/frameable work of art, dancing, drumming, and designing a self-care plan.

In 2012, we began offering Befriending the Body—trauma-sensitive yoga groups for clients—as an adjunct to our counseling program. The professional and allied members of the direct-services community voiced their interest in participating in customized classes for themselves. Previously ignored or underserved communities of color, monolingual Spanish speakers, and seniors celebrated our effort to make yoga accessible. The response has been tremendous and it is becoming our third earned-income social enterprise.

CONCLUSION

Direct services are the hallmark of most nonprofits. Our services are in large part delivered by passionate, idealistic, energetic, and socially conscious people who want to make a positive contribution to humanity and, in their small way, change the world. And, if an agency offers trauma services, it is imperative that leadership recognizes its role in supporting workers and in creating structures that will sustain them.

CHAPTER 2

Understanding Vicarious Trauma

It has been many years since various researchers (McCann & Pearlman, 1990; Pearlman & Saakvitne, 1995b; Figley, 1995; Stamm, 1995) have given us the construct of vicarious trauma. Research literature has documented the negative aftereffects of the cumulative engagement of bearing witness to the traumatic material of clients. We have literature that speaks to caretakers, clinicians, medical personnel, disaster recovery/relief workers, and hotline advocates.

WHAT IS THE DEFINITION OF VICARIOUS TRAUMA?

The literature has proposed and used interchangeably a handful of concepts and terms such as *burnout, compassion fatigue, compassion stress, secondary traumatic stress, secondhand shock,* and *vicarious trauma* to describe these aftereffects. These terms have slightly different or overlapping catalysts and symptomatology. All are rooted, however, in the result of empathic engagement with trauma stories or other materials belonging to victims/survivors.

WHAT DOES VICARIOUS TRAUMA LOOK LIKE?

Is it just occupational stress that can be relieved by a good night of sleep, a hot bath, a couple of slow nights, and a long weekend or two weeks of vacation? Hardly.

MY STORY

In Chapter 1, I told you about my agency and the myriad of services the organization and my staff members offer to our clients. Now I'll relate my story and how I personally came to understand how important self-care is for all staff members, from interns to the most senior executive.

I had been working in the field of crime victim assistance for five years when I realized the trauma that I was absorbing from clients' experiences was qualitatively different from the "stress" my best friend was experiencing in her high-profile corporate database marketing firm. She was weary of doing the same thing, day in and day out. She likened it to being chained to a conveyor belt in a factory. She spent all day processing paperwork and sales orders, inputting consumer profiles, and deflecting sexist and racist jokes.

We shared our workweek woes. And we dissected our isolation as "lone women of color" who were frequently asked to represent, explain, or excuse viewpoints from communities of color.

We both looked forward to the local old-school midweek happy hours that would last until the club closed at 1 a.m. We took "mental health days" when we couldn't bear another day in the office. We were both experiencing classic symptoms of burnout. My friend was bored, operating on autopilot, and had lost all enthusiasm and zest for her job. For her, it was simply another day and another dollar. On the other hand, I was experiencing physical and emotional exhaustion. I had little emotional energy left for anyone or anything at the end of the week. I was rapidly gaining weight and too tired to think about doing anything but figuring out which comfort food would satisfy me.

Our work worlds were starkly different. My symptoms were the result of empathic engagement with the trauma material of crime victims. And, too often the crime victims resembled me: a single, African-American woman. My job involved listening to my clients' experiences of robbery, aggravated assaults, sexual and domestic terrors, and losing a loved one to homicide or suicide. *My work became my life.* I found myself avoiding particular neighborhoods or locations. If for some reason I had to visit a particular establishment, I found myself envisioning the crime that had taken place there. Yet, I excelled in my position, and within three years was promoted and given administrative responsibilities that included managing other counselors.

I had mastered the "fake it till you make it" mode of operating to an award-winning level. I quelled intermittent anxiety by delving into my new management activities, and pointed to my overwhelming workload when friends wanted to do something more relaxing. I was surrounded by colleagues who normalized my experience by stating:

- "Yes, I understand; I'm on too many committees too!"
- "You're fine; it just takes getting used to this kind of trauma."
- "This is what it takes to be recognized and succeed!"

Recognizing My Vicarious Trauma

It was a textbook case of secondary traumatic stress. I was hyper-vigilant, a bit numb, and worst of all, my sleep was affected. I was off-kilter, and I knew it. I continued to ask questions by conferring with a group of community mental health professionals who had formed a mental health collective designed to mentor and support graduate students and professionals of color. Their consensus of what was going on with me: a mild case of vicarious trauma.

They disagreed with my victim service colleagues. I *would not* be fine if I neglected to address the historical trauma and other root causes, and it was imperative that I develop healthy interventions. They inquired about my physical, emotional, and spiritual supports. They asked if I was experiencing intrusive imagery, heightened distrust, and if I felt vulnerable or out of control. They wanted to know about my connections to family and friends, and if I felt a sense of intimacy with my supporters.

I began reading about the difference between burnout, compassion fatigue, and vicarious trauma. While I was out of balance, my worldview, operating assumptions, and beliefs about the basic goodness of the world had not (yet) changed. I had many of the same symptoms as people who suffered from vicarious trauma, as well as another significant cognitive challenge: They questioned their worthiness, along with the benevolence and meaningfulness of the world. Hmm, this all sounded familiar. I pondered conversations in which a few of my victim service colleagues said things about their clients, things that were mean, ugly, and full of contempt.

During the late 1990s, I attended a series of support groups designed to provide a space for program and executive directors to network and garner support. Everyone was experiencing an alarming rate of staff attrition, increased use of sick time, and numerous workers' compensation claims resulting from accidents. Clinical supervision had disappeared or was being conducted by inexperienced graduate interns. Gossip, triangulation, and conflict plagued the agencies. Morale was weak. The profile/leadership of one crisis center had badly deteriorated and was frequently the topic of negative speculation by all of the others, resulting in the loss of community confidence, collaborations, and funding.

Soon it felt like a club of members who felt misunderstood or alienated from their own agency. These particular "club members" were totally disillusioned with their career choice ("I hate social work!"), and this view colored their daily social interactions. They were resentful when asked by clients, staff, or funders to do something different (for example, improve collaborations, diversify funding, address their lack of ethnic/cultural capacity, develop a better business or strategic plan, or provide a more meaningful impact-driven evaluation).

The clusters of symptoms I was observing in my colleagues, and in myself, began to make sense. Pearlman et al. were correct. Our years of empathic engagement with the trauma of survivors had changed us. (McCann & Pearlman, 1990; Pearlman & Saakvitne, 1995b, p. 71; Figley, 1995; Stamm, 1995). I personally would be financially set for life if I had a dollar for how many times a colleague (who I believed was suffering from vicarious trauma) rationalized any of the following:

- "Cathy, you don't understand. I am a manager/executive/team leader and *I have to work* 50- to 60-hour weeks."
- "Sure, I have gained weight. I eat lots of fast food because I am too tired to cook."
- "I try to avoid people when I am not at work. The world is sick. This damn work is not for the faint of heart. Cathy, people are crazy."

I dropped out of the club and the networking group. Also, I wanted to address a broader spectrum of needs for communities of color and there were only a few organizations that had *a person of color* on staff. I needed to distance myself from the chronic complaining and problem-focused group that took the "isn't it awful" game to new heights.

My Journey to Self-Care

I developed the individualized self-care program in late 2003. At the onset, my idea to create a wellness plan was simply rooted in a convergence of my life experiences. As the executive director for CTR starting in fall of 2001, after having been an employee for 10 years prior, I witnessed scores of staff members, not only in my own organization but in the nonprofit sector at large, succumb to secondary traumatic stress and vicarious trauma. Vicarious trauma is often seen as a normal byproduct of important yet stressful humanitarian work whose impact on occupational, social, and personal arenas often goes unrecognized.

What I know for sure is that every day, whenever someone calls or walks through our door, that person or someone he or she loves has been traumatized by crime. Staff will be called upon to listen, counsel, support, advocate, broker, and fully engage in the recounting of that person's trauma experience. The strain on staff members is immense and immeasurable. My responsibility includes ensuring that our clients and staff feel safe, remain stable, and are able to thrive in this environment. Much of my professional work has been influenced by Ms. Byllye Avery, a healthcare activist who has dedicated her life to improving the physical and emotional health of low-income African-American women using the vehicles of peer support, self-help groups, and advocacy networks. As founder of the Avery Institute for Social Change and The National Black Women's Health Project (NBWHP), Ms. Avery, through the "active promotion of emotional, mental, and physical health," has challenged the misconception that health is merely the absence of physical illness. In the program's early years, its signature methodology was the SisterCircle, a peer-support health group.

In the early 2000s, I attended a local conference, during which one of the keynote speakers, Loretta Ross, a staff member of NBWHP, challenged the Denver participants (and conference hosts) to begin a peer support group. A health advocacy organization, NBWHP was founded on the premise that black women needed a vehicle to address how negative social and economic factors aggravated their health. Peer support groups became an organizing vehicle and safe place to discuss holistic health. Several months later, I received an invitation to attend an organizing meeting for a Denver peer support group. At that meeting, 12 African-American women expressed interest in forming a group. That is how my own Denver SisterCircle was born. We met on Sunday afternoons, one Sunday a month, for 10 years! Through this transformative experience, I learned to engage with other women around issues of health as a member of a group, instead of the person facilitating a group. I learned how to be vulnerable, share power, engage rather than avoid conflict, and experiment with alternative modalities for healing. While the support group was all about us as individuals, it was never *just* about us. It was about how to impact the health of our larger community as a model, a light, a guide, and a vehicle to increase wellness. My SisterCircle experience provided the catalyst and insight to develop a comprehensive self-care program for my agency.

During this period, I received an advanced degree in medical anthropology. I was mesmerized by the relationship between health, lifestyle, and culture. In particular, any discussion of primary, secondary, or tertiary prevention—reducing exposure to health hazards, screening and detecting at-risk activities, and eventually intervening to reduce disability and acclimate people to their environment—was fascinating. I marveled at the strategies communities put into operation to survive.

I agreed with psychiatrist and anthropologist Arthur Kleinman's approach to healthcare as integrated and intrinsically social. (Kleinman, 1981). The explanatory model offered a culturally responsive approach by focusing the concern on the affected individual and his or her community. I distilled his eight primary questions into four that resonated with me as a service provider in the field of crime victim services:

- What is the problem?
- How is it the problem/illness interpreted?
- What problems has it caused for the individual or community?
- What treatment/strategies can be accessed to help an individual/ community get well?

I was working in the field of trauma and crime victim assistance. Subsequently, I completed an advanced degree in social work. I had notebooks full of "tips" for coping with workplace stress. I had attended periodic "how to manage your stress" seminars. Why wasn't it working?

Something was very wrong. I continually witnessed bright, capable colleagues despairing and leaving the field. Others were so cynical and jaded it was impossible to get any innovative work done. We were in a helping profession, and *we* needed help. We had perfected "learned helplessness" and defended the construct. Then, I had a brainstorm. Why not implement a holistic plan to take care of ourselves? The perfect coalescence of my peer support group experience and graduate school education, in both medical anthropology and social work, enabled me to blend the healthcare policy camps of health promotion and health protection.

HEALTH PROMOTION VS. HEALTH PROTECTION

Health promotion policy lays the full weight of a healthy life in the hands of individuals. Health promotion advocates advance beliefs that healthier ways of living occur through better nutrition, regular exercise, and avoiding or tempering smoking, alcohol, gambling, driving too fast, and so on, as a means to reducing life stressors.

Health protection advocates suggest that the responsibility for many stressors is rooted in political and economic disparities. They reveal that the role of environmental pollution (not just literally, in the form of pesticides and noise, but in the glamorization of fast food, as well as lack of fresh produce stores, walking/bike paths, and affordable, modernized recreation facilities) and unequal distribution of resources (higher education, health insurance, etc.) make healthier living almost a middle-class luxury. (Ratcliffe, Wallack, Fagnani, & Rodwin, 1984).

CONCLUSION

In the chapters that follow, I share the employee self-care program that began in 2003 at The Center for Trauma & Resilience in Denver, Colorado. I begin with a discussion of our celebrated health-promoting individualized self-care plan, then speak to health-protection strategies that provide the foundation for the individualized self-care plans' realization. Throughout the book I use real-life examples to illustrate challenges and successes that I have encountered in creating the self-care program. The names and identifying details in these examples have been changed to protect the individual's privacy.

CHAPTER 3

Understanding the Vital Reasons for Adopting an Individualized Self-Care Plan in Your Nonprofit

The three main reasons for a nonprofit executive to adopt an individualized self-care plan are to:

- prevent being consumed by our work and making burnout, secondary traumatic stress, and vicarious trauma a "badge of honor";
- stem the tide of staff attrition, turmoil, chaos, and ultimately, the dismantling of programs or nonprofit agencies; and
- recognize the toll that this type of work takes on staff and leadership alike.

PREVENT STAFF BURNOUT AND SECONDARY TRAUMATIC STRESS

The first reason a nonprofit leader should institute an individualized self-care plan in a nonprofit organization is to prevent staff members from being consumed by their work and making burnout, secondary traumatic stress, and vicarious trauma "badges of honor."

Organizations award merit badges to people who have made themselves sacrificial work warriors. We can call them *badge-of-honor members*. This philosophy is right in line with the long hours worked in the United States.

Badge-of-honor members feel compelled to be available at a moment's notice. One of my colleagues stated, "When I travel, even out of the country, I make sure my staff can contact me 24/7. I am always there for them!" Badge-of-honor members eventually report chronic exhaustion and feeling irritable, aggrieved, and often overwhelmed.

- "I feel like I am the only one who does anything around here!"
- "I don't trust most of the people I work with."
- "I would rather do it myself than depend on anyone else."

Badge-of-honor members rarely set limits or boundaries. An employee stated, "My former domestic violence shelter supervisor scheduled supervision on a Sunday, during brunch, so she could legitimately drink mimosas!" Common comments include:

- "I have never had time to take a real vacation; someone always needs something. In fact, I worked most of the major holidays last year!"
- "If I don't (plan the party, put up the decorations, update the protocols, order the supplies, repot the plant, repair the chair, arrive early and stay late), then nothing gets done around here!"
- "If I leave, I am afraid things will fall apart while I am gone!"

These employees resent and belittle people who leave when the day is done. They are unkind with colleagues who regularly schedule vacations and have a life outside of crisis work. The complaint list can be endless— just like the excuses. Staff members who set boundaries and maintain them may hear comments such as,

- "Are you requesting time off again?"
- "Wow, I wish I had time to (enroll in an art class, go to the gym, take a vegan cooking class)!"
- "Are you only on two committees? I guess you are not really interested in advancing here."

REDUCE STAFF ATTRITION, TURMOIL, AND CHAOS

The second powerful reason nonprofit leaders should institute an individualized self-care plan in their nonprofit organization is to stem the tide of staff attrition, turmoil, and chaos that can ultimately dismantle our programs or nonprofit agencies. As trauma service providers, we see firsthand how fatigue, unresolved conflict, and poor judgment become the norm in agencies.

We are constantly recreating the wheel or lack energy to innovate. There is environmental disorganization and little institutional memory. I have heard comments such as:

- "Where is that (DVD, software, laptop, iPad) equipment we purchased last year?"
- "We missed our proposal deadline, by 15 minutes. I can't believe they would not accept it!"
- "We are too overloaded to deal with another demographic … homeless victims."
- "We don't have time to evaluate our programs; we are too busy serving clients."
- "I don't know the history or purpose of 'xyz,' and who cares now?"

In my tenure, three Denver executive directors of nonprofits have sought my counsel and mentorship. They shared with me their extreme frustration with their staffs and boards. One stated that she felt "as if I am being held hostage." All three asked me to consider merging their programs under mine. They were financially strapped and unable to retain staff more than one year. Their boards had very different ideas and endeavored to remain afloat. All three executives resigned their positions after the first year of their employment.

In a three-year period, 2007–2009, CTR provided volunteer training curricula to a local community-based mental health center no fewer than five times. Each time we provided that center's newest coordinator with our advocacy curriculum, we inquired about the previous employee and the location of our donated materials. Not one of the five new employees had any idea that we had provided our curricula or support to a previous employee.

The pattern repeated itself with another agency in 2012. My agency received a request for "technical assistance" and was asked to meet with the program director of a local domestic violence shelter. There was conflict between how the program director wanted to run the program and how the volunteer coordinator wanted to do things. We spent an intense day working with them to help resolve the conflict. Six months later both individuals had left the agency, and we received another call from the new director requesting the same "technical assistance."

Rampant staff attrition becomes an issue for affected agencies. The door revolves so rapidly that the community feels the breeze as services stall. Internally, there is incessant finger-pointing among members of the board and staff resulting in excessive resignations, poorly handled dismissals, and unceasing public skirmishes between current and former staff members. Colleagues become reluctant to partner on collaborative proposals or silently withdraw support from the spiraling organization. Management effort to contain the disorder further isolates the agency as it implodes. Telephone calls go unanswered, organizational correspondence is ignored, and donors are neglected, or worse, forgotten.

Real-Life EXAMPLE

I have a friend named Phyllis, a donor and former board member for a sexual assault nonprofit. She and I served on the board together. In fact, she donated half the amount of money the organization needed to purchase its permanent home. The building was purchased and housed the nonprofit. However, due to rapid executive turnover (five times in about five years), donor records and relationships disappeared. Phyllis, who was the agency's longest-term and most generous contributor, was no longer invited to agency events, fundraisers, or recognitions. She eventually ceased making donations. She said to me, "Well, clearly they were no longer interested in me or money . . . so I just stopped giving it to them."

RECOGNIZE THE TOLL THAT THIS TYPE OF WORK TAKES ON US

The third reason a nonprofit leader should institute an individualized self-care plan in a nonprofit organization is to recognize the toll that this work takes on everyone. We operate on autopilot and denial. We exist on minimal sleep, fast food, over-the-counter medications, and little exercise. Our physical health is compromised by weight gain or loss, chronic fatigue, hypertension, and a weakened immune system. A former employee said to me, "The stress was so high at my previous job that I began losing weight so rapidly I thought I was going to disappear."

Emotional ideations span from periodic insecurity, such as,

- "Did my dress look pretty at the open house?"
- "Why didn't anyone ask me if I wanted to go to happy hour?"
- "I think XYZ is the program director's favorite!"

Emotional ideations can also lead to feelings of persecution:

- "I never get recognized for all of my good work."
- "I get penalized for being assertive and speaking up."
- "I think Cathy dislikes me. She never compliments me, engages me, or supports my ideas. She doesn't even look at me. She is hostile and wants me to resign."

Staff members become chronically dissatisfied, procrastinate, ruminate, manipulate, and routinely threaten to leave the agency, the profession, and the nonprofit sector altogether.

The idea of fun becomes an obligatory chore or is relegated to "happy hour drinking with co-workers." We would rather hibernate than attend a celebratory event. We just send a check in the mail instead. We don't have the energy to plan a dinner party or night out at the theater. We have forgotten how to play chess and have not danced, biked, bowled, or gone skiing in years.

We realize that we haven't read an association journal for years; in fact, we don't remember what a best practice looks like anymore. We think that whatever we learned about our discipline 10 years ago is sufficient. We attend conferences to get "a little rest and relaxation" and hope no one asks which workshop we attended! One colleague stated, "Our young, new director is like the Energizer bunny. She doesn't realize people stopped working two years ago!"

We look bad, feel bad, behave badly, and think everyone else is the problem.

CTR'S INDIVIDUALIZED SELF-CARE PLAN—GOAL AREAS

CTR's individualized self-care plan is holistic, addressing the body, mind, and spirit. The plan asks employees to create *stretch goals* in five areas of their personal life: physical, emotional, financial, intellectual, and spiritual. Stretch goals require a little more effort and may require alterations of your daily routine.

Physical

We feel compelled to work long days, some evenings, and weekends. We barely exercise and eat on the run (and in our vehicles) or cram calorie-laden sugary snacks at our desks. It is rumored (and my personal experience and observation lead me to believe that the rumor has validity) that for every year a worker spends in the human services or trauma services field, that individual will gain a minimum of three pounds. Other health risk factors include headaches, stomachaches, backaches, insomnia, blood pressure flare-ups, and digestion issues (from acid reflux to constipation). These worn-out immune systems result in staff members and leaders having more than our share of colds, infections, flu, allergen attacks, malaise, and overall fatigue.

Emotional

We are the ones with whom others leave remnants of their trauma, baggage, and emotional "junk." Our own emotional health can be easily thrown off balance, especially if we have our own personal trauma history. We appear aggravated, have angry outbursts, and feel frustrated and misunderstood. We begin obsessing over petty issues, collude with other pessimists, and discard our problem-solving skills. Eventually, we miss appointments, meetings, and grant proposal or report deadlines. We disengage, disbelieve, and begin blaming our mistakes on clients, co-workers, or other professionals. Our poor choices get us into trouble, and we constantly dream about "getting away."

Financial

We compromise or neglect our financial health. We postpone saving or accessing financial plans and overuse our credit cards. We believe that we do not make enough money to save, and conversely (often out of guilt, since our clients often earn even less), overspend on items that give us momentary comfort like alcohol, recreational marijuana, fast food, jewelry, makeup, tattoos, collectibles, or body products that purport to help us to relax, revive, and rejuvenate. We soon realize the product can't deliver and we have just added more debt and clutter to our homes and offices.

Intellectual

We learn how to do our job and then become complacent. Our volunteer program, agency programs, and board trainings are antiquated. We don't pursue new literature or research, or learn about emerging or promising practices. Coupled with physical fatigue, we neglect hobbies and dismiss opportunities to expand or delve into new activities. We are adamant that there is nothing new under the sun. We are recalcitrant and competitive with allies. We coast by attending the same conferences year after year and never consider an allied or complementary field. Unfamiliar with the landscape around us, we rely on television to educate us. We bury curiosity and resent implementing any new idea or any request to change.

Spiritual

We bear witness to horror, terror, criminal intent, insanity, inhumanity, and injustice. Our work tests our belief in the goodness, value, and meaningfulness of the world. We are weary from the racism, classism, homophobia, and other micro-aggressions directed at us, personally or at our work. We flirt with ethical dilemmas and then rationalize our unethical behavior. We minimize impact by comparing one crime or tragedy with another. We wonder if benevolence exists. We have heard and seen devastation. We become guarded, distrusting, and have ceased to believe in miracles. We see little value in having a spiritual life.

CONCLUSION

Over the years, I experimented with other categories of self-care. However, after supervising and listening to dozens of employees, I came to realize that these five areas offered the most flexibility in definition and interpretation.

Getting Your Nonprofit Started on Individual Self-Care Planning

One of the first and most important conversations that leadership at the staff and board levels should entertain is whether the agency is ready to fully, sincerely, and wholeheartedly begin the journey toward agency self-care.

I was formally introduced to the concept of readiness as a student in medical anthropology where we were encouraged to explore alternative health systems in ethnically and culturally diverse environments. We had to be ready to accept social, environmental, and biological factors that influenced health or illness in the context of the whole community. Later in my career, readiness was a concept featured in the work of The Denver Foundation's *Inclusiveness at Work: How to Build Inclusive Nonprofit Organizations*, which asked nonprofits to begin a readiness assessment before they begin to take on the issue of diversity and inclusiveness in their agency.

The task of developing and integrating a self-care plan into the infrastructure of an organization requires leadership to be open to the inevitable policy and program changes that will occur. Leadership must be willing to look at themselves and their agencies with new eyes. Genuine readiness will sustain you through the challenging times, so that you can stay the course in the midst of everything that can and will happen while guiding your agency toward health.

Chapter 4 focuses on the most common questions nonprofit executives ask me about compliance, privacy, and legal issues surrounding a self-care program, and then describes how to get started implementing individualized self-care plans for their organization.

FREQUENTLY ASKED QUESTIONS ON IMPLEMENTING SELF-CARE

Three of the most commonly asked questions from nonprofit executives about implementing individualized self-care plans in their agency concern:

- **Compliance** —"Have you ever had someone refuse to participate in the plan?"
- **Privacy** —"How do you handle an employee who says that self-care is a private matter and none of your business?"
- **Legality** —"Are you breaking any laws?"

Staff Compliance

Over the past 12 years, there has been only one employee who refused to participate in our agency plan after he was interviewed and hired. The following is a brief snippet of what occurred.

Real-Life EXAMPLE

Edward was a newly hired employee who believed that our self-care policy was frivolous. During his first week of employment, he became irritated during the self-care plan orientation and demanded to know why we were requesting that he disclose personal information. He became insubordinate with his supervisor and refused to entertain or comply with the expectation. Edward demanded a meeting with me, the executive director of the agency. He was inconsolable, became outraged, and alleged "harassment" when I informed him that the requirement had been presented in the job posting and interview and was, indeed, part of his job description and was not negotiable. I appealed to his intellect and clinical ethics and gave him data from the research literature that documented vicarious and secondary traumatic stress as an "occupational hazard, a consequence of knowing, caring about and facing the reality of a client's pain, endured as a result of traumatic events." (Pearlman & Saakvitne, 1995). I shared that the literature offered promise: staff members that make time to sustain relationships and do basic self-care tasks seem to be less at risk for the negative effects of caregiving. He remained obstinate and flatly refused to participate. After several reasonable attempts to enlighten him (and after consulting with our human resource attorney), he was separated from the agency.

Our self-care requirement is a standard objective in *every* agency job description, and our philosophy is incorporated into each new-hire interview. To instill the sincerity of our commitment, interviewers for new hires discuss the inherent stresses of working in a trauma-serving agency—regardless if the candidate is applying for an administrative or clinical role.

During the interview we discuss our board-sanctioned self-care philosophy and job description, which requires each staff member to create an annual plan for self-care.

Because the interviewee may already be taking self-care steps, interviewers are encouraged to ask candidates to identify any strategies they currently use to cope with and manage stress. The responses received over the years generally fall into three categories.

- One-third of the candidates assure the interviewing team that they "manage stress very well." They disclose that after a "crash-and-burn" experience, they have learned to "avoid stress."

- The next third state that they have not given any serious thought to their strategies or confess they know "stress management" is important and that they plan to do better in the future.

- The last third typically report activities such as physical exercise, reading, praying, or taking a vacation "when it gets really bad!"

The literature has reported that many trauma-serving organizations are deficient and irresponsible in preparing, training, and supervising staff on aspects of vicarious traumatization. Supervisors and managers should focus on early identification. "Interventions need to be multi-level and the interventions should not be left up to the individual alone." (Figley, 1995; Meichenbaum, 2007, p. 11). Lipsky & Burk state that organizations themselves have the potential to either mitigate or exacerbate the effects of trauma exposure for their workers. (Lipsky & Burk, 2009, p. 21).

Concerns About Confidentiality

The second most common question is, "How do you handle employees who state that their self-care goals are too private to share with you or the agency?" *Confidentiality is paramount.* I cannot stress strongly enough the importance of this ethical code. If there is a breach, it does not matter how benign—there will be no second chances with supervisees.

An individual's self-care plan must not be shared with anyone else without his or her explicit permission. One slip and the individual employee's equilibrium will be compromised. One slip and the whole program may be at risk. Reestablishing balance is central to the CTR philosophy of self-care planning. I recommend that employees' self-care goals be kept in their personnel or other confidential file that is secured with a password or locked.

Of course, an employee is able and welcome to share his or her individual goals. Oftentimes many are eager to provide examples to inspire newly hired employees. It is not unusual to hear staff proudly exclaiming on their progress or citing the method they used to accomplish their goals.

Nevertheless, it is important to reassure staff members that their goals are confidential and will not be shared outside of supervision without their permission. On occasion, during presentations, examples of self-care may be anonymously presented. If any staff member determines that his or her goals are too private to share, then those particular goals remain private. There is no mandate to share goals.

Some goals may be easier to discuss with supervisors than others. In my experience, employees may have several goals they want to strive toward; *they decide* which one they want documented for their annual performance review. An employee's plan may encompass a number of wellness and self-care activities. Staff members do not need to feel overly burdened by listing everything that they intend to do to maintain a healthier lifestyle.

The requirement is to identify one goal. If a staff member is reticent about sharing any goal, that individual can choose another and keep the perceived difficult one as a private goal on his or her own personal-best list. Some employees have shared their ambivalence about sharing a personal desire or vulnerability. They vacillated in identifying the goal because they wanted my thoughts or support.

Real-Life EXAMPLES

Della privately discussed wanting to undergo a voluntary sterilization procedure, but had some fears she would be judged.

Marino wanted to locate and/or learn about his biological parent. He expressed anxiety and trepidation about even entertaining the process.

Darla had been unsuccessful for two years in her attempt to teach a group fitness class. After our discussion, she concluded that she no longer wanted to work on this goal.

Staff may fear failure, and that a failure may negatively transfer to their overall feelings of self-worth if they are unable to attain the goal. Self-care goals are intensely personal, and thus striving to achieve a goal can warrant success as much as achieving the goal. I coach staff that "learning" can still occur during the process of striving.

Leadership Concerns About the Plan's Legality

The third most common question posed to me is, "Is this self-care requirement a violation of any employment contract or law?" Human resource professionals have advised me to carefully consider any job requirement to prevent straying into an area that appears to elicit information that could be discriminatory in any manner. If you decide to draft a similar policy, have it reviewed by legal advisors. Our board-sanctioned policy states:

The Center for Trauma & Resilience values staff contributions and future successes. Towards that end, the self-care program is required for all employees to help mitigate vicarious and secondary traumatic stress, which are inherent when working in an environment with victims of trauma and crime. Vicarious trauma is considered to be an occupational hazard, a consequence of empathic engagement with others' traumatic material. (Pearlman & Saakvitne, 1995). As part of the self-care plan, employees will create their own personal objectives in five areas. Employees will then be internally supervised on their progress, both monthly and yearly, as part of employee performance reviews. The self-care plan is not an attempt to elicit performance on staff abilities or disabilities. The self-care plan is a requirement for all staff, not just counseling staff. Our administrative, finance, human resource, and development employees participate. No one is exempt, not even the executive director.

IMPLEMENT INDIVIDUALIZED SELF-CARE PLANNING

My overarching goal for employee self-care and creating a wellness environment is to promote mindfulness, learning, and balance that will sustain us in our quest and service for social justice. I believe that an investment in wellness helps fosters resilience in a field where we know trauma exacts a toll. As Audre Lorde stated, "Caring for myself is not self-indulgence, it is self-preservation, and that is an act of political warfare." (Lorde, 1998, p. 131).

Self-Care Planning Begins on Day One

On the first day of employment, new hires are reintroduced to the concept of self-care. During their initial 30 days of employment, they create annual (pro-rated) self-care goals in the five areas outlined in Chapter 3 (physical, emotional, financial, intellectual, and spiritual).

The concept of self-care as part of a job description is foreign to everyone I have hired since the plan's inception. Therefore, I start with a warm-up exercise during which staff members are asked to complete a self-awareness narrative, an exercise borrowed from my graduate foundation social work class. The Presentation of Self exercise asks the new hires a series of questions designed to bring them awareness about "how they show up in the world." It asks them to identify their strengths and areas for improvement in various areas of their life. It asks how others may perceive them and if these perceptions are congruent with their own perceptions or if they may be interfering in personal or professional relationships. This exercise sets new staff members on the journey toward what I have deemed "enlightened self-care."

Without fail, if employees had already begun a self-care proposal prior to the narrative exercise, the original proposal is trashed and replaced with a new proposal. It is at this point that new employees often express astonishment. They become both excited and apprehensive.

- "Am I really going to use work time to create this exercise?"

- "Do I have to write down what I want to accomplish?"

- "This assignment is more difficult and more stimulating than I imagined."

The Final Self-Care Plan Should Be Well-Crafted and Reflective

A self-care plan is not simply a list of tips on how to relax. It is not a toolkit of quick fixes like buying yourself flowers, having a cup of herbal tea, lighting an aromatherapy candle, laughing at a joke, or going for a quick walk around the block. It is not another how-to-be-happier book or DVD, gathering dust on shelves or buried in an electronic file.

The individualized self-care plan is well crafted, requiring reflection and serious contemplation. The final product becomes part of each employee's annual performance evaluation.

Stretch Goals vs. Maintenance Goals

I promote the development of stretch self-care goals instead of maintenance goals. A *maintenance goal* may be a routine activity like attending a weekly spiritual or religious service. Maintenance activities are likely something the employee is already doing. A *stretch goal* may be to audition and sing in the choir, teach a spiritual lesson, begin a new aspect of the ministry, visit another spiritual tradition, or volunteer for the church food pantry. Stretch goals may require a year to accomplish, literally or psychologically. The questions employees may ask while crafting their goals are:

- What goal do I want to accomplish?
- How will I achieve this goal?
- How can it be measured?
- What will be different when I accomplish my goal?

It is important to note that the individualized self-care goal may involve others, but to ensure success should not be *wholly dependent* upon others. For example, if a selected goal is to have monthly date/activity nights with a partner or family member, it is important to get that person's agreement before attempting this endeavor; otherwise, the plan may not succeed.

Ending or Beginning an Endeavor May Be the Goal

The individualized self-care plan may involve beginning a new endeavor, or it may involve ending one. Self-care is not always about adding something to our life. It may require subtracting. If someone is overwhelmed, dissatisfied, or just plain bored with an activity (or a relationship), he or she may choose to give it up. New endeavors may require a number of steps, which is perfectly acceptable when crafting goals.

Real-Life EXAMPLES

Angelle was a smoker who wished to quit. She knew it might take some time for her to give the habit up. Therefore, her self-care goal for the first year included attending smoking-cessation classes, wearing a nicotine patch, or trying electronic cigarettes if that didn't work.

Camille identified that she spent too much time with nonreciprocating friends. She decided to give up initiating social activities with these friends and joined a "Denver MeetUp group" to get acquainted with new people and participate in (at least) six new social gatherings.

Jessica was overcommitted and overwhelmed with multiple projects, family obligations, and volunteer activities. For her self-care plan, she decided to set a deadline to formally resign from some of her volunteer activities and focus on only one project.

Goals Are Submitted, Reviewed, and Approved

After employees design their goals, they submit them to their direct supervisor for discussion, review, and approval. Once final goals are solidified, they become part of the check-in for employees' supervisory meetings, progress reports, and annual performance reviews.

Newly hired employees are often challenged with the idea of stretch goals and rattle off things on their to-do list. "I want to (clean my house, attic, car, garage)." Or an individual may offer vague, esoteric items like, "I want to (laugh more, be happier, be less guarded/defensive, or have peace of mind)." Whereas these goals may be admirable, they may not necessarily be stretch goals and are difficult, although not impossible, to measure. It may take a few weeks of discussion to help the staff member create meaningful and measurable goals. Don't begrudge them the time.

Confiding with Confidence and Measuring Goals

Supervisors and supervisees should work together to find a measurement system that is mutually agreed on. While there will be some amount of trust (honor system) necessary, all goals should be measurable (or on occasion demonstrable) and results-oriented. For example, if an employee decides that her intellectual goal is to take 12 vegetarian/vegan cooking classes, there are many ways to measure this goal. The staff member can show the supervisor a receipt for the cooking classes, bring 12 dishes to the office for sampling, or reduce her weight, blood pressure, or cholesterol levels as a result of carrying out this new skill. On occasion, if requested, supervisors may offer self-care suggestions for supervisees.

Real-Life EXAMPLES

Jason was a young man who had relocated to Denver and joined a new spiritual tradition. He stated that he feared his choice would be discovered and deemed unacceptable by his parents, who practiced a more conservative tradition. I encouraged the young man to consider writing a letter to his parents and to send them literature and Internet links about his choice. He agreed and added the letter-writing goal under *"spiritual self-care."* And while it took him six months to write the letter, he eventually accomplished his goal.

(Continued)

Gina was a portrait artist using paints and oils. She wanted to get more exposure for her art and supplement her income. During supervision, we discussed exhibiting her work at local nonprofit fundraisers. She sold two paintings in one year. She accomplished this goal under *"financial self-care."*

Lisa disclosed during supervision that her own home "was modest" and that she was not comfortable hosting friends or celebratory events in her home. The following year I introduced her to an acquaintance who was a professional home organizer. Together they renovated and redecorated her home. She accomplished this goal under *"emotional self-care."*

Supervisors should encourage staff to dream, freely share examples, and explore goals that nurture and strengthen their supervisees. As supervisors get better acquainted with the capacities of their supervisees, they may gain a better insight into the abilities of those individuals to stretch. Staff members who intentionally underplay goals may benefit from guidance and reassurance. I have learned that with a little coaching and supervision, superficial ideas are cast aside and more genuine interests replace them. Ultimately, self-care goals are selected by the employee and should be honored.

It is not unusual for staff to underestimate the amount of time and energy required to commit to and successfully arrive at their destination. For example, one staff member who had been employed with the agency for more than six years chronically shared her wish to lose 20 pounds. Year after year she accomplished four of her self-care goals—all except this one. Finally, I suggested in supervision that she focus only on her physical goal and disregard the other four areas of self-care for the entire year. Reenergized and conscientious, she was able to lose twice the amount of weight in her original goal! Supervision can help staff to remain focused. It is vital for motivation and stamina.

SUPERVISE THE PLAN AND MANAGE RESISTANCE

It is vital that the leaders of the organization supervise the plan and manage resistance whether it come from employees, volunteers, or interns.

The integrity of the program requires that management at every level uphold its virtue.

Supervising Self-Care Goals for Staff Members

Once the goals have been determined and documented, employees are held accountable for their original goal. It is not unusual for staff to "get cold feet" and want to reconstruct their goals. Predictably, this occurs approximately two weeks to two months after the goals have been crafted. Employees may obtain new information after they write their plan—and everyone has to cope with that dynamic.

Goal flexibility or expansion

On occasion, a staff member may request to expand his or her goal because the individual accomplished it quickly. This may be a sign that the goal lacked appropriate stretch. Enhancing a goal is acceptable, but scrapping it altogether is discouraged. I learned very early in our practice that constant revisions, whether in the first month or in the last quarter, are a management nightmare. The "I changed my mind" or "I don't want to do that now because of . . ." can be avoided by carefully inscribing the goals from the beginning. It is not unusual for "life to happen," and within two or three months a staff member may decide under *"financial goal"* that she wishes to *spend money* on getting dental braces instead of *saving money* in a mutual fund. Certainly, there is nothing prohibiting the employee from accomplishing both. However, the original agreed-upon and documented goal is the one for which the staff member will be held accountable.

It may be tempting, but supervisors must hold firm. Needless to say, while some flexibility may be in order, too much is discouraged. The program will lack validity if it doesn't hold the same rigor as other components of their job description. *Learning to be accountable to oneself is part of the self-care process.*

Monthly goal review

Each month during supervision, performance goals for program/administrative/self-care areas are discussed and reviewed. After a couple of months, if supervisors notice that supervisees have not made any progress or are postponing, frustrated, or slipping on a goal, they should not shy away from having a pointed discussion. If supervisees need to vent, whine, problem-solve, or brainstorm, all avenues may be productive in helping them realize their goals.

Following is one of my conversations with a supervisee who became resistant and oppositional regarding one of his selected self-care goals.

Supervisee: *"I changed my mind. I stated that I wanted to read 12 books, but now I want to read six and begin volunteering to mentor a student instead of reading all of those books."*

Supervisor: *"We have already discussed your goals at length, and we have agreed upon the goals you suggested."*

Supervisee: *"I know that. I have been thinking about it . . . and after all, it is my self-care plan and I think I should be able to change it."*

Supervisor: *"Yes, it is your plan. We have agreed upon the plan you suggested. The original plan is the one that will be evaluated."*

Supervisee: *"I can't believe this . . . Self-care is important to me. I know what I can do and what I cannot do. Isn't volunteerism important in this agency?"*

Supervisor: *"It's only February. We didn't discuss the type or length of the books you agreed to read. Perhaps you can read a few children's books and you can still reach your goal. Of course, volunteering is much admired, but it was not your original goal and you will be evaluated on the goals we agreed upon."*

Supervisee: *"I don't read children's books."*

Supervisor: *"I was making a suggestion. What kinds of books were you anticipating reading? How can you make more time to read? Or, you can give up on the goal entirely. It is up to you."*

Supervisee: *(after a long sigh)* *"I guess I will try to get this done."*

Over the years, these types of argumentative discussions have been atypical, but I have concluded they are cloaking a myriad of other employee performance issues (as was the case with this particular employee). This dialog typifies the kind of back and forth that will happen if anyone is unclear at the outset of the plan how it will be evaluated.

The employee chose the goals and then reneged. Supervisors may already be aware of discontented and disgruntled staff and should realize that having individualized self-care plans will not prevent those issues from surfacing or dissipate them. In fact, if the self-care plan seems a bit outrageous—as in the case of one pregnant employee who wrote that she intended "to climb a Fourteener mountain"—it may be a clue that the employee is less than invested and an exit is imminent.

Supervising Self-Care Goals for Volunteers and Interns

Our agency, like the majority of nonprofits, relies on volunteers and interns to provide a variety of direct services. Our volunteers and interns primarily support counseling staff in the delivery of crisis and support group services. As with employees, we have included a self-care component in the volunteer job description, and it is a requirement for placement at our agency. A portion of our 40-hour agency training is dedicated to educating and preparing volunteers for secondary and vicarious trauma. Interns who are asked to make a weekly commitment of 8 to 16 hours per week for a minimum of six months are pleasantly surprised that they will get academic credit for taking care of themselves.

And, as with employees, interns receive individual as well as group supervision. Still, resistance may arise among the ranks, particularly if an intern is struggling to meet internship requirements. The following is an example of a discussion between one intern and the director of training and volunteer programs (DTV).

Real-Life EXAMPLE

The intern, Priscilla, had missed several appointments at the agency. She had been advised and warned, and eventually her educational learning plan and weekly internship schedule were restructured. Two weeks after

(Continued)

the new plan was implemented, Priscilla and the director of trainings for volunteers had the following conversation during their regular biweekly supervision.

DTV: *"Hi, how are you? How is your new schedule working?"*

Priscilla: *"I'm okay. I want you to know that I was pretty upset with you when I left your office a few weeks ago."*

DTV: *"Oh? I am sorry to hear that. Why were you upset?"*

Priscilla: *"I thought you were punishing me . . . that you didn't like me. I kept vacillating about quitting this internship altogether."*

DTV: *"I am glad we're talking about it now. Neither of those things is true."*

Priscilla: *"I know, I know. I mean, I know now. After you asked me to look at my schedule and make some difficult choices, I had to give up some things and delay a few things . . . I didn't want to give up all the things I was doing. Then, my husband and my kids and I had the best weekend we have had in several months. We went out for breakfast, we played outside in our backyard, and we watched movies together. On Sunday night, my husband said, 'So if this is self-care, I like it!' No one has ever taken time or even cared about me enough to tell me I was trying to do too much."*

DTV: *"I am so happy that it is working for you!"*

Our intern program asks for a minimum commitment of 8 and maximum of 20 hours for six months. The director of training and volunteers routinely receives requests from interns to extend a six-month term to a full year. Additionally, our agency participates in an intern pipeline program that hosts students who represent disenfranchised racial, ethnic, and linguistic populations. Historically, the pipeline hosts had to agree to interview all interns for employment positions if they met (and were interested in) the criteria for any open position.

Since its inception more than 15 years ago, 11 former interns were hired for entry-level positions. One former intern stated that The Center for Trauma & Resilience had raised the bar for her prospective employers.

She was unable to find a nonprofit employer who had "an authentic self-care program."

INVESTED SUPERVISION ADVANCES SELF-CARE SUCCESS

Several years after implementing our individualized self-care plan, I was reunited with former employees who had relocated out of the city or accepted another nonprofit program position. The first thing each one disclosed to me after our mutual greetings was their level of stress and dismay that they were no longer formally (and actively) practicing self-care.

I felt like a failure. My desire was to effect a lifestyle change and I believed that I had not been successful. They consistently responded to my encouragement to continue to practice self-care plans in their new environment by stating, *"Cathy, we know how to do it, we are trying, we just don't have any support (or incentive) for doing it! It just doesn't feel the same!"*

I realized something. I wasn't a failure! They were aware and knew the benefits of self-care. During these conversations with former employees, I learned that regular supervision provided opportunities to guide, model, honor, champion, and make recommendations to staff. And, indubitably, a supervisor's authentic interest and investment were named as key ingredients for success. Supervision *was* a lynchpin for success.

CONCLUSION

It is a compliment to be consulted and even more of a compliment to be invited to make recommendations and have them accepted. I remain in awe of the trust that has been placed in me over the years and know that it is a privilege to be invited a bit more deeply into the lives of employees.

Investing on an individual level is a "feel-good" exercise. The employee and supervisor have the potential to be winners. How does it fare across the organization? What are the system tools we implemented to make it work?

CHAPTER 5

Evaluating the Self-Care Plan

In "Managing Oneself" (2005), Peter Drucker, a guru of organizational management, states, "Organizations are no longer built on force but on trust. The existence of trust between people does not necessarily mean that they like one another. It means that they understand one another. Taking responsibility for relationships is therefore an absolute necessity. It is a duty." (Drucker, 2005, p. 9). To augment its value and significance, self-care goals are included in every employee's annual performance reviews and *equally* weighted with other performance indicators such as administrative, fundraising, technology, business, clinical, or program goals.

MANAGEMENT BY OBJECTIVES EVALUATION SYSTEM

Many evaluation systems are used for employee performance reviews. Currently, we use our modernized version of Peter Drucker's Management by Objectives (MBO) evaluation system, which includes a reflective assessment of stated objective and goals. (Drucker, 1954). Employees are asked to share the highlights and challenges of their year and make recommendations for professional or personal growth. According to Drucker, employees must be seen as assets and not liabilities. Employees who are encouraged to participate in the organization's strategic-planning process and have a clear understanding of what role they will play in the delivery of the goals are more likely to become engaged and empowered employees.

Remember that the measurement process and outcome for an employee's individualized self-care goal are not predetermined and may be constructed in hundreds of ways. It is essential to enlist ideas about how the individual's result-oriented goals will be measured. Following are a few examples.

- Hilary was interested in establishing a walking regime. She was not interested in measuring her weight loss. She purchased a pedometer and kept a weekly walking journal.

- Patrice selected a similar activity and decided that her measurement tool would be to ultimately participate in a 5K charity walk before the year's end.

- Frederick decided that he would establish a walking club and would lower his blood pressure by five points by year's end.

All of these employees were substantially overweight. However, the agreed-upon outcomes were very different for the same activity. Certainly, if someone is overweight, it may be tempting to encourage that individual to create a "weight-loss" goal. Resist the temptation, because such a suggestion would dishonor the process and devalue the employee.

The outcomes may be unusual. One of the most unusual measurement tools came from an employee who wanted to stop drinking orange soda. "How will I know that you have been successful?" I inquired. She stated, "I won't be late for work for a whole year, because I won't be up until midnight (as a result of drinking orange soda all day and night)." While this was an unusual and seemingly small physical goal, it put her on the path to better sleep and hydration and prevented future performance improvement notices about her tardiness.

NUMERICAL RATING SCALES

Many evaluation systems have numerical rating scales. Figure 5.1 is an example of the tool that we have used with employees. Self-care goals are incorporated into the MBO scale.

Staff members may choose to create more than one goal for each of the five categories (physical, emotional, financial, intellectual, or spiritual). However, performance is required and measured for only one (pre–agreed-upon) goal. Figure 5.2 is a sample case study asking how one would numerically rate an accomplishment and how to think through and rate the actions of the employee.

FIGURE 5.1 ■ Numerical Rating Scale

The scale rates the employee's performance between 1 and 5.

5 Outstanding . . . . .The goal was exceeded by twice the original (or in spite of extraordinary odds!).

4 Very Good. . . . . .The goal was exceeded by one-half or in spite of extraordinary circumstances.

3 Achieved . . . . .The goal was accomplished.

2 Needs Improvement . . . .The goal was partially accomplished.

1 Not Achieved. . . . . .The goal was not accomplished.

FIGURE 5.2 ■ How Would You Rate the Following Accomplishment?

An employee stated that his financial goal was to save $1,000 and place funds in a savings account. At year-end, the employee had saved $500. He stated that due to unforeseen vehicle repairs, he was unable to save an additional $500. During monthly discussions, as the supervisor you are aware that there *was* an attempt to save the funds but unforeseen circumstances hindered the person's performance. The goal of $1,000 was not obtained. Obviously, a rating of a 5 or 4 is unlikely. In our system, the staff person would probably receive a 2 rating or "needs improvement." I know what you are thinking . . . vehicle repairs (and many other financial snafus) are unpredictable! Life is unpredictable! It's not for the lack of trying!

I agree. However, how the employee is progressing toward the original goal would be a topic of discussion during monthly supervision. How can the employee still obtain the goal despite unforeseen obstacles? Together, the supervisor and supervisee generate ideas such as bringing lunches, giving up daily lattes, and delaying the purchase of a new electronic toy. Employees do not need to become derailed by circumstances "beyond" their control.

Well, you might say, that makes sense *if the obstacle occurred during the first quarter*. Although the worker planned to save money, ultimately he was unable to save because he had to repair or purchase a car. Perhaps the goal to save money may need to be modified—not abandoned altogether.

Okay, that's understandable, you may say, but what if the unforeseen obstacle occurs *in the last quarter or month* of the annual evaluation? Again, I would say devoted supervision is the key. If the goal is absolutely impossible to attain, then refocus by encouraging a 5 rating in another area to balance out the inevitable 2 or 2.5 rating. It is important for supervisors to convey to employees that getting a poor rating in one area will not totally dismantle an annual performance review.

COPING WITH STAFF DISAPPOINTMENT

Staff members who get stuck or are unable to accomplish their goals may become resentful and upset about the agency's self-care requirement. It is not unusual for anxiety to set in a few months before the close of the evaluation period. Staff members typically respond in two ways. They either sprint to the finish line or give up entirely and receive a comparable evaluation score. If employees choose to give up, the supervisor may anticipate irritated statements like:

- "I don't care. I take care of myself in other ways."
- "Why do you care?"
- "Why is this any of your business anyway?"
- "I didn't want to strive for xyz in the first place."
- "Well, I guess it is another lesson learned."

Employees may offer a bunch of justifiable excuses and rationales. "Well, my passport didn't arrive so I was unable to travel to London . . . so I took a staycation for two weeks." Wonderful, but that was not the identified and agreed-upon goal. Some individuals may share their personal disappointment or embarrassment. Others pout, blame, haggle, or become tearful. Empathize, but remember that their goals (and the measurements) are self-selected.

Of course you may allow employees to rant (as long as it remains respectful), and then evaluate them accordingly and move on. An invested response could expound on the role of self-care and the hazards of vicarious trauma, sympathize with any obstacles, and ferret out the barriers while working with employees on creating new goals for the upcoming year.

Real-Life E X A M P L E

Paulina was unsuccessful in four of five of her self-care areas. She pretended that she was making progress during monthly check-ins with her supervisor. She was unable to document her results at the end of the year. During a discussion with her supervisor, she realized that every goal on her plan involved spending money. She was not able to secure extra funds, and thus her plan failed. She gained new self-awareness and insight on creating realistic self-care goals for the next year.

If employees give up on a goal, supervisors have no choice but to evaluate accordingly. I typically state unabashedly that I have seen firsthand the effects of vicarious trauma and defend our diligence to prevent it. I empathize, and then I move on.

Thankfully, the irritated resistance conversations have been rare. After many years of supervising individualized self-care plans, I have observed that with each succeeding year, the majority of employees steadily reach to progressively extend themselves. Employees have shared with me that knowing they will be supported and held accountable increases the likelihood of accomplishing previously *perceived* unobtainable goals. And, if supervisors are able to garner and maintain staff trust, they will learn that staff members will surprise themselves and perform in wondrous ways.

Real-Life EXAMPLE

I recall one employee, Dahlia, a single parent, full-time employee, graduate student, and prominent community volunteer with a neighborhood church. Dahlia had two children who were academic scholars. One was involved in the dramatic arts and the other in ecological endeavors. Even in today's world of jam-packed schedules, they continued to have a family dinner together (at the dining room table) every night. During her third year of employment, Dahlia solicited my assistance with her "emotional" self-care goal. I suggested that she plan a real vacation, versus only taking time off to write/finish papers. I suggested she plan two vacations—one with her children and one without. I can still remember how she gasped (quasi-offended) and stated, "Impossible! You have no idea how difficult that would be for me!" A week later, she reported, "It would have been unthinkable before coming to work here, but I agree, and I want to do it." And she did!

I encourage supervisors to allocate the time for longer individual supervision sessions. On supervision day, a conventional workday will be shorter. The supervisory conversations tend to be delicate and more profound as employees gain perspective of themselves and the world around them. Previous supervisory sessions that were composed of questions such as "What should we serve for the volunteer lunch?" or "How many times can I switch schedules with my co-workers?" and "Can I reorder art supplies for the children's group?" will be a thing of the past.

A pleasant surprise for leadership may be that less and less supervision time will be spent on "minutia and mechanical" concerns and more time on creative and visionary plans they have for themselves and/or the agency.

KEEPING LONG-TERM EMPLOYEES ENGAGED

Employees who have been with an agency for several years may seek inventive approaches for self-care plans. During the course of my writing this book, there were five employees who had been with CTR for more than 10 years. When I asked each about his or her historical perspective, all stated that they felt "stretched, accomplished, and challenged by the practice of self-care!" Several years ago, I stumbled upon a few resources to enthuse staff members who had been with the agency for more than five years.

Use Books and Articles for Inspiration

While shopping at a local family-owned market, I found a magazine article that imagined "52 Weeks of Self-Care." It had a wide array of inexpensive and simple activities that promote overall health. I gave this article to interested employees. The article required individuals to relinquish control and adhere to whatever arbitrary assignment was recommended. For example:

- Week 1—Buy someone flowers.
- Week 2—Try a new piece of fruit (star fruit, mango, kiwi, Asian pear).
- Week 3—Clean out your junk drawer.
- Week 4—Give up sugar.
- Week 5—Write a poem, and so on.

I scanned my bookcase and found a list of books dedicated to self-care endeavors (for example, *All the Joy You Can Stand, The Happiness Project, The Art of Happiness, The Four Agreements,* etc.), and gave the books or ideas presented in them for employees to consider in the creation of future self-care planning.

To date, my longtime favorite resource came from an article in *Ebony* magazine. It was a whimsical article, entitled "The Top 40!" It was a list of the 40 things you must have (or have given up) by the time you reach that age. See examples below.

---

1) Peace of mind (and piece of property). 2) A will. 4) A savings account in your own name. 12) A sense of humor, style, and purpose. 18) A library card (used often). 19) A credit card (used sparingly). 23) A cause célèbre (domestic violence, infant mortality, save the whales — your choice). 25) A personal trainer. 26) Selective amnesia (What Saturday morning meeting?). 28) A good skin care regimen. 31) A pair of silk pajamas. 39) A dream.

I redesigned it to be appropriate for individual employees. On occasion, I ask staff members to create their own list of a dozen experiences or ventures to fulfill by the end of the year.

Real-Life EXAMPLE

One employee, Jean, wrote the following:

1) Try a new haircut or style. 2) Sing karaoke in public. 3) Select an international charity and donate. 4) Read an autobiography. 5) Submit my DNA to find out my country of origin. 6) Purchase a pair of silk pajamas. 7) Write a love letter. 8) Turn off the television for a month. 9) Attend a social justice rally. 10) Create a signature recipe dish. 11) Buy a savings bond. 12) Take a dance class. 13) Plant an herb, flower, or vegetable garden.

A tenured (19 years!) employee, Kathi, decided to make a self-care list of 100 things that made her happy. She set out to intentionally seek "happiness" throughout the year. The documented items spanned all five categories of the agency's self-care plan. How cool is that?! By year-end, she had accomplished 88 out of the 100 items. Although she had not completed all 100 items, she reveled in the fact that she had done a number of activities several times, such as attending outdoor summer concerts, making three quilts (instead of one), and hiking three Colorado trails.

SELF-CARE PLANS EDUCATE AND ENERGIZE EMPLOYEES

I can attest that the majority of employees report they are energized and enthusiastic about self-care planning. And, regardless of their actual evaluation score, they discover something novel about themselves. They actively ponder and embrace the need to prioritize their own health and enlist the people in their lives, such as partners, adolescent children, colleagues, and friends, to help them achieve their self-care goals. Following are some examples of individual staff members' goals in each of the five categories and how they accomplished them.

Physical Goals

Typically this is the first and easiest goal for individuals to identify. In the last five years, one staff member lost 43 pounds while another young male staff member who wanted to build muscle did so and gained 10 pounds. Another individual resolved an ongoing acute medical issue. Others achieved a variety of physical goals including joining a bike club, a recreation center, and a group fitness class with a personal trainer. Other staff members completed a series of yoga/meditation classes. One learned to swim. Another stopped smoking (breaking a 20-year habit). One person hiked 12 trails; one went swimming with dolphins; another lowered her blood pressure by 5 points and her cholesterol by 20 points. Two staff members trained and ran in a half marathon, another became a vegetarian, and one learned to belly dance.

Emotional Goals

These goals usually require some explanation and coaching. One person conquered her fear or phobia (bridges) and walked across the Royal Gorge

Bridge in Colorado. Several staff members (new parents) established custody/guardianships. Dozens planned 12 partner "date nights" (that didn't involve food or movies). Two completed a family genogram. Some began therapy, AA, or Alanon meetings. Some scheduled mini-vacations each quarter, while others went off the grid for a weekend. One individual participated in a 10-day silent retreat. One individual had cosmetic surgery and updated her wardrobe by purchasing 12 new outfits a year. Another framed all the art prints she had stashed around the house.

Financial Goals

There is the ever popular "I want to save money and pay off a credit card," which some employees did. Others enrolled in a budgeting class, purchased a used car with cash, hired a financial advisor, and bought or sold a home. One staff member organized an investment club. Several began donating to an international charity. One started a savings fund by marketing and selling her artwork. One identified 10 new ways to save money and another raised her credit score 10 points. One employee decided she could no longer afford her pets, so she gave them to someone who could.

Intellectual Goals

This is a goal that asks staff members to explore learning in an area that has little to do with their day-to-day job. A number of staff members have enrolled in graduate school. One read six Shakespeare plays, another 10 books off the *New York Times* Bestsellers/Oprah book list. Some organized book/independent film clubs, while another organized a local boycott. One wrote a short story, several enrolled in language or yoga/meditation classes, and another took voice lessons. Several visited local art galleries, one attended restaurant tours, and two signed up for cake decorating. Several staff members resigned from boards/committees/groups. One learned to play poker, three became Zumba instructors, while others enrolled in learning a variety of new skills, from piano to carpentry.

Spiritual Goals

We define *spiritual* as any goal that uplifts, brings joy, and creates a greater sense of community. Spiritual goals have been interpreted in the following ways: taking yoga classes, doing meditation, hosting quarterly dinner parties, learning how to camp/backpack alone in the wilderness, planting an urban garden, stop/start going to church, joining a community choir, taking dance lessons, or playing a musical instrument. One person began volunteering for a local food justice organization. One person, terribly unhappy with her birth name, chose a new name and legally changed it. Another staff member submitted her DNA to find her African ancestry and country of origin. And one of my favorites: a mother and daughter chose tattoos. The mother's says "You are my sunshine," and her daughter's says "My only sunshine"!

STAFF REFLECTIONS ON SELF-CARE—Three Testimonials

The best way to show how our self-care program has benefited and inspired staff is to hear from them directly. To share the power of self-care, I want to share with you three testimonials—each in the employee's own words.

Testimonial 1

Staff member Janice (10 years of employment at agency)

I remember Cathy introducing the self-care concept to me as my clinical supervisor in 2003. At first it was difficult to even think about taking care of myself, as I had little time for taking care of three kids, helping run my husband's business, and focusing on supporting a struggling nonprofit. The first experience I had with self-care helped my feelings of guilt fall away each time I took time for myself away from my family, whether it be spending time with friends or going to a movie by myself.

A little background—my parents provided my three brothers and me with every opportunity we thought we needed or wanted (within reason— again the guilt thing) and were very helpful in caring for us. You could say we were very good at self-care as adolescents and teens—even into our college years—as we were very individualistic and perhaps self-centered. We had the financial self-care piece down, care of our father, as well as the spiritual piece (myself in particular while trying each denomination until I felt spiritual—not sure if that would hold true now). The intellectual piece was incorporated into our higher education. Emotionally, my parents were strongholds, and I was open with them (even if my brothers weren't) about my ups and downs. They were in-house therapists in many ways. Physically I played many sports, continued to make better times on swim team, and became a better soccer player each year.

Then adulthood hit, and very soon after, parenthood. Instead of taking the path of continuing my self-care, I took on the role of what I thought a mother should be (and wife for that matter)—a selfless supporter, even financial provider at times. I also married a person who came from a collective society—what is best for the family and society rather than what is best for the individual. Because I had been spoiled and self-serving, this new role came with regret at times, rebellion at others, and of course anger.

Then I met Cathy, and I had to become aware that if I were to be a provider to a community and a provider to a family, I needed to be whole and healthy. To get there I needed to become self-aware, without being self-centered. I needed to talk about my needs, ask for what I needed, and model for my daughters (and sons) what a parent and leader might look like—even if I am only a leader in my family, or only a leader in my workplace. The guilt excuse was old. The time excuse was even older.

Over the years I have become very successful with four of my five goals. The fifth goal around physical issues has been the most difficult. Again, I had it easy in my youth—fairly successful at each of the five goals without much work or sacrifice because of my extraordinary parents. My weight will continue to be a struggle, but I will continue to work on my self-care goals around health, as that is the highest indicator of my resiliency to stress, my outward representation of leadership, and if (when) successful, it will be my true example of self-love. As they say, if you can't love yourself it is very hard to be able to truly love another. Even though my physical self is only a piece of my existence, it is a very important one.

Testimonial 2

Staff member Kathi (19 years of employment at agency)

I kept most of my self-care goals since 2003 and took some time to review them. It really was a walk down memory lane. Looking over 10+ years, there clearly were some lessons that I needed to learn to really understand what self-care is about and why it is so important.

Lesson 1: I am a worthy priority. An early theme in my plan was how to make myself a priority, and what it cost when I didn't. *"I feel resentful when I don't get to the gym. This leaves me acting passive aggressively with my family. This leads to guilt and frustration."* I took a few rides around the carousel before I learned this one. I felt too demanding. I felt selfish. I felt like I should be able to do more. I felt like a bad mom, wife, daughter, when in truth, when I took the time to take care of myself, everyone was really happier. If I had diabetes no one would say, "Skip your insulin, I need you to run to the bank." Well, when dealing with compassion fatigue (complicated with a PTSD diagnosis) that pretty much is what I am doing when I skip the gym to wait for the plumber. We all learned to work together to make everyone's schedule a priority. We work around, not over the top of, each other's schedule.

Lesson 2: I don't have to do everything I am invited to do. Maybe it's because I am a people pleaser by nature, or it was good for my ego. If I was invited to be on a committee, be on a board, volunteer for a project, or go out to dinner, I felt like I had to accept. Today, this doesn't mean that I don't do any of the things that I am invited to do, but I think it through. I weigh my options and don't automatically say yes. This allows me to not feel resentful about doing things I don't want to do, and it allows me to have time that I need to do the things that I want to do.

Lesson 3: Feeling poorly affects how stressed I feel; too much stress results in my feeling poorly. Duh! Hmmm, the number of sick days I used reflect my overall health. I blamed it on having kids in school, I blamed it on shopping carts, and I blamed it on changes in the season. Yes, all these things can make me sick, and they did. But when I am on top of exercising, eating healthy, washing my hands, and not feeling overwhelmed, I tend to stay well. Proof for me was fever blisters . . . I get stressed, I get one. Self-care has reaffirmed for me the mind–body connection. Do I get sick? Yes . . . but a lot less than I did in years past.

Lesson 4: Planning is so much better than reacting. There really is such a thing as a resiliency bank. Even when I am making my self-care plan, I am planning on how I am going to get it done and choosing things that are going to help my resiliency. It's not just checking things off of the list. It's the process of doing them and benefiting from them. Planning when I am going to exercise, scheduling exercise as an appointment that carries the same weight as my other appointments, not just when I can squeeze it in. All these things make a difference. Sometimes life throws me a curveball and I have to react. Fortunately, this is when the resiliency bank kicks in, and I have the resources to make it through.

Lesson 5: Self-care is not the same thing as New Year's resolutions. I make New Year's resolutions *in addition to* my self-care plan. Sometimes I get to them, sometimes I don't, but they are not the equal. I spent years confusing the two. I would put my self-care goals on my New Year's resolution list and beat myself up when I didn't get to them. Now I look at them differently. Self-care is about enhancing my resiliency; it is about taking care of myself in order to be able to do the trauma work that I do and not let the work cost me my health, my family, and my spirit. My New Year's resolutions are things that I have come up with after looking over my past year that I feel will improve who I am, how I am, and the environment that I live in. If I neglected my self-care I was not very successful at my New Year's resolutions.

Lesson 6: Support is the key. I probably should make this number one! In the words of Sir Elton John, "I thank the Lord for the people I have found." I am blessed with an incredible group of very supportive people. People who know me well enough to see when it's not going well and help me come up with a plan to do it differently. People who are willing to be part of that plan have been put to the test! If you have a work environment that supports self-care and embraces shedding the "badge of honor," that's ideal. But you probably won't or won't always have that

(Continued)

environment. Self-care is about you, for you, by you. And you do it with the support of those who care about you. No one can do it for you, and you need to do it whether it's part of your work environment or not.

Lesson 7: Identify what makes me happy and do it. This has been my favorite lesson. It clarified for me why I do self-care and how I have benefited. I embraced making my quality of life a priority, and it made it crystal clear how those around me benefit from it. It is a proactive plan that involved making a list and making the time to do the things on the list. I didn't wait for opportunities to present themselves, I made them. I stopped doing the things that didn't make me happy. I learned a good lesson in transformation. Growing up, I did not believe I had any artistic ability. I was a left-brain girl, not very creative unless it had to do with the math and sciences. My left brain needed to do things in the most efficient way possible, which led me to my right brain (along with my kids' love of arts and crafts). I figured out I that I could do a few things myself, like make a flyer or design a costume. I really enjoyed it. I started purposefully working out my right brain and met a whole new side of myself that brought me much joy and happiness.

Lesson 8: It really is for me, not for my evaluation. My goal-oriented, people-pleaser personality and need to succeed got me started. The results kept me going. Sure, I think I am a better, more functional employee as a result, but I am also a better, happier, and healthier person as a result. I have a part-time job with a large health system that primarily cares about my getting to work and getting my job done. The people I work with are great and I enjoy the work, but self-care is not something on the corporate radar. I am not evaluated on my self-care goals; I doubt that they even know I have a self-care plan.

Lesson 9: Sometimes you do everything right and life still kicks your butt. The good news is that when I have been taking care of myself, I can get back up. Sure, sometimes it takes a minute. But I recognize what being triggered feels like, and I know what to do about it. I have skill and tools which help me, and I don't have to drag myself up from the bottom.

Lesson 10: I do have time. I think this is my biggest pet peeve because I used to believe the opposite. When I began my first self-care plan, I had two children, a husband, parents that lived close by, a house, pets, friends, a part-time job, and a very needy lawn. I thought that there was no way I could squeeze one more anything into this full and busy life. I also had anxiety, depression, trouble sleeping, and a fierce startle response. It was the badge that I wore to honor all the good work that I did. Creativity, boundaries, and compassion for myself and wanting to do better for my family drove me to find a way to practice a more intentional self-care. Addressing my sleep problems didn't take any more time than having them . . . in fact it took less. It turns out my whole family enjoyed going for a walk after dinner, and it eased quite a few symptoms and provided another outlet for family time. I still have two kids, a husband, pets, friends, and a needy lawn. My parents are older and require more time and care. I commute three days a week, one hour and 15 minutes each way. I still have a part-time job. I figured out how to do everything differently, and I have time because I prioritize and value my self-care.

Testimonial 3

Staff member Claudia (4 years of employment at agency)

The idea of self-care was very foreign to me. Coming from a country where rest and self-indulgence are not the norm, it was difficult to assimilate the concept of caring about myself. In Mexico you are expected to work hard and care about your family and to leave your desires last.

Living in Chicago was not different. A metropolis filled with foreigners with similar backgrounds, the expectations seemed strikingly similar, especially working at a nonprofit organization. Furthermore, I remember when I visited the director of the social work department at Jane Addams College of Social Work, she made a statement that I can't forget: *"In social work every day is different, but in this field you will be overworked and underpaid."* My career and cultural background stem from a philosophy that encourages putting it all first before you, even clients.

That was a reality for me until I came to work for The Center for Trauma & Resilience. During my first interview I was asked what I do for myself. At

(Continued)

that time I didn't comprehend why doing something for myself mattered. Four years later I have learned the importance of valuing yourself, your time, and still having a strong work ethic.

Most mental health workers get burned out and overwhelmed with cases. Having a self-care plan allows me to be compassionate in the field. On a regular basis I rely on the various activities that I have set for the year. Having the ability to reach out to a place, a time and a space that allows me to be with myself, that reenergizes me, that reminds me that the work that I do is important and caring for me is just as important as helping others.

I know I can be a caring professional, one who has boundaries and gives herself the necessary tools to constantly be refreshed and renewed. I inevitably compare my life as a counselor in Chicago and Denver. Even though our cases are far more violent and tragic, I am able to focus on striving at delivering services while finding a balance between work and personal life.

That homeostasis I believe differentiates us from other nonprofits. Our executive director, Cathy Phelps, is strict, yet considerate and appreciative of our work. That environment enables staff to feel appreciated and to want to give more of ourselves and to participate in new projects. Equally amazing is the fact that we incorporate that philosophy with our clients. We educate those who come to us about the importance of being healthy, exercising, eating well, making effective choices, etc. Having a holistic approach that begins at an internal level allows us to convey our mission and it makes our work authentic.

USING METRICS TO BACK UP THE ANECDOTAL

Do we have statistics to back up the anecdotal descriptions of the self-care benefits? You bet we do!

In 2011, the director of training proposed that we begin to survey staff utilizing the Professional Quality of Life (ProQoL) instrument. It is the same instrument we use in our vicarious trauma workshop and would later become one of the evaluations we used as part of our trauma-sensitive yoga classes. She distributed the scale electronically, and all answers were anonymously submitted to Survey Monkey. The scale rates Compassion Satisfaction (CS), Burnout (BO), and Secondary Traumatic Stress (STS). The ProQol instrument defines these measures:

Compassion Satisfaction (CS) is about the pleasure you derive from being able to do your work well. For example, you may feel like it is a pleasure to help others through your work. You may feel positively about your colleagues or your ability to contribute to the work setting or even the greater good of society. Higher scores on this scale represent a greater satisfaction related to your ability to be an effective caregiver in your job.

Burnout (BO) Most people have an intuitive idea of what burnout is. From the research perspective, burnout is one of the elements of Compassion Fatigue (CF). It is associated with feelings of hopelessness and difficulties in dealing with work or in doing your job effectively. These negative feelings usually have a gradual onset. They can reflect the feeling that your efforts make no difference, or they can be associated with a very high workload or a nonsupportive work environment. Higher scores on this scale mean that you are at higher risk for burnout.

Secondary Traumatic Stress (STS) is an element of compassion fatigue (CF). STS is about work-related, secondary exposure to people who have experienced extremely or traumatically stressful events. Developing problems due to exposure to others' trauma is somewhat rare but does happen to many people who care for those who have experienced extremely or traumatically stressful events. For example, you may repeatedly hear stories about the traumatic things that happen to other people, commonly called vicarious traumatization. If your work puts you directly in the path of danger, for example, fieldwork in a war or area of civil violence, this is not secondary exposure; your exposure is primary. However, if you are exposed to others' traumatic events as a result of your work, for example, as a therapist or an emergency worker, this is secondary exposure. The symptoms of STS are usually rapid in onset and associated with a particular event. They may include being afraid, having difficulty sleeping, having images of the upsetting event pop into your mind, or avoiding things that remind you of the event.

During the last four years, our numbers rank lower than the national average for burnout and compassion fatigue—BO 16 (22), STS 16.4 (22)—and our compassion satisfaction is one point higher than the national average—43 (42).

CONCLUSION

Witnessing firsthand, having a tool to measure quantitative data, followed by staff testimonials about the positive impact engaging in self-care has on their lives inside and outside of the office, is heartening. While I believe it is a positive and proactive leap, it will not eliminate all personnel or human resource concerns.

CHAPTER 6

Self-Care Plans: The Magic Wand or a Human Resources Panacea?

Oh, how I wish I had stumbled upon a magic elixir and cure-all for vicarious/secondary trauma and potion for employee sustainability! Unfortunately, offering a program on self-care for the workplace is not magic for all that ails agency personnel.

Nonprofit employees, as employees in any work environment, bring personal and professional experiences—both positive and negative—to their place of employment. On occasion, some employees transfer their anxiety, grief, anger, and wariness of leadership/management compounded by psychological bruising from previous occupational skirmishes to their current workplace. In addition, employees may bring specific characteristics or personality features that thrive on ego, stealth, manipulation, and self-importance. They may hide their feelings of incompetence by attempting to intimidate and deceive management and/or engage in conflictual and inappropriate behavior.

A problematic employee may aim to use the agency's health and wellness philosophy to further self-absorbed goals. A self-care policy should not be used as an excuse or rationale for neglecting one's job responsibilities or exploiting agency resources.

ENSURE PRIORITIES ARE CLEAR

Clarity is key. The mission and business of the agency is the priority. Matter-of-fact and seemingly (to some) mundane items are first and foremost:

- Getting to work

- Getting to work on time

- Attending to self-awareness

- Consistently producing a quality product, report, or experience for clients and co-workers

- Accommodating and accepting (even if one disagrees) management decisions

- Attending to self-regulation

Even in an agency with self-care protocols, employees are not exempt from being given performance improvement notices for tardiness, absenteeism, missed deadlines, ignoring management directives, exploiting agency resources, safety violations, or a poor quality-assurance performance. As shown in the following real-life examples, vigilance must be taken to ensure that the concept of *self-care* does not mutate into *self-centered care*.

Attendance

Getting to work *and* getting to work on time are crucial for the agency to do its business.

Real-Life EXAMPLE

Cora was convivial and had many years of clinical social work experience, but her personal disorganization interfered with her getting to work. She called in "sick" so often during her first (and only) year of employment that within six months she had expended 108 hours of leave time (sick and vacation). She provided a variety of reasons, including misplacing her keys; claiming that a freshly painted apartment interfered with her ability to sleep well; feeling stiff because her cat slept on her legs; being distraught by the morning news broadcast; and so on. Cora was supervised, accommodated with a flexible schedule, and eventually offered a four-day week. Yet, her chronic absenteeism continued. When she was separated from the agency, she had only worked one complete month in a 12-month period.

Tardiness

Getting to work on time is as important as leaving work when the clock strikes 5:00!

Real-Life E X A M P L E

Nedra was charismatic and competent in her administrative role. After a few weeks of unaddressed tension with her conflict-avoidant supervisor, she began arriving to work three to ten minutes late. This pattern continued until she was given a performance notice. Nedra requested to speak to me (as executive director) instead of her supervisor. She stated that she was angry and taking it out on her supervisor. She saw her supervisor arrive late, so why couldn't she? She questioned how her supervisor could demonstrate the same pattern of behavior, but didn't appear to be in trouble. I informed Nedra that personnel matters were privileged and confidential. And if her supervisor were in disciplinary trouble, she would not be aware of it. I recommended that she concern herself with her own performance and encouraged her to speak to her supervisor about the unaddressed tension between them. She agreed that her solution had been a poor choice.

Self-Awareness/Self-Management

Poor emotional intelligence skills, which can include lack of self-awareness and self-management, can quickly deteriorate an agency's environment.

Real-Life EXAMPLE

Fidel was educated in the field of social work, yet appeared to have little self-awareness or ability to regulate his behavior. If he became disappointed or frustrated by events in his personal life, it was conveyed by sullen, moody, and distancing behaviors with co-workers and interns. His behavior became hugely problematic, especially after his unsuccessful attempts at dating others in the agency. When the relationships ended, he became disrespectful to his prospect. His behavior caused an outcry of "harassment" and triggered an investigation. Fidel was unable to restrain himself. Because he was unable to sense or understand his environment, he became defensive about how others reacted to his behavior. Soon, however, his lack of self-awareness and self-management collided with his ability to respect management and work within a team. He was separated from the agency.

Self-Management Regulation

Staff members must be able to self-regulate their behavior instead of acting out and behaving as if every environmental change or imposed boundary is a personal affront.

Real-Life EXAMPLE

Victor was a part-time employee. He worked full time for a large government agency where he had little control over his workday. After missing several jointly scheduled meetings with his supervisor and neglecting to turn in his timesheets, he was given a performance warning. When his careless behavior continued, he was placed on probation. He became upset. He called and left irate messages for his supervisor alleging that he was a beleaguered worker. In every instance where he had missed an appointment or did not complete an assignment (including self-care assignments), he cried "foul play." He blamed everyone else for his shortcomings. Eventually, he was separated from the agency.

Quality Assurance

Internal quantitative and qualitative evaluations complement and validate your services.

Real-Life E X A M P L E

Shelly had shared that she felt traumatized by her previous work environment. She initially reveled in the self-care philosophy and took advantage of supervision, workshops, flextime, and any extracurricular development opportunities. However, she had trouble tracking, documenting, and staying organized. She became increasingly anxious when her performance faltered. Instead of stretching to address these issues, she complained to co-workers and attempted to antagonize and triangulate management. She consistently offered excuses for her inability to perform.

Real-Life E X A M P L E

Annabel had worked for a large, bureaucratic organization. She was often "lost in the shuffle" there, so she had difficulty comprehending how attuned our agency was to protocols regarding quality assurance and case management documentation. Annabel struggled with case management and case documentation. Her supervisor provided additional training, along with a "cheat sheet/checklist," but her performance didn't improve. Annabel was counseled and her employment probation period was extended.

ENSURE STAFF DO NOT EXPLOIT THE WELLNESS PHILOSOPHY

There are a number of human resource scenarios that prove to be taxing for management. Although they are a bit bewildering, the following are rare, but real-life examples of individual employees' attempts to exploit the wellness philosophy and goodwill of the agency.

Real-Life EXAMPLES

Giselle impulsively left the agency after taking her one-hour lunch break because she decided she needed an "emergency massage" in the middle of her workday. She was given a performance notice and had two hours deducted from her vacation leave.

Barbara was pursuing her social work license. After four months of employment, she requested that the organization pay the biweekly clinical consultant to provide her weekly supervision. In this way, Barbara reasoned that she could more quickly fulfill her required social work supervision hours. Her request was denied and she resigned shortly thereafter.

Valencia wanted to attend her daughter's weekly swim and dance lessons (not a recital or competition) during work time. Her request was denied. Several months later, she requested to "have the summer off." This request was also denied and she resigned.

Zee had been an intern with the agency and applied for a staff position. He mentioned that he was working several jobs trying to make his private practice work. After being employed for two months, he began making requests in order to accommodate his other part-time jobs. His requests were denied. Later, he requested referrals for his private practice and then for his practice partners. Four months into the position, he resigned. Upon his exit, his supervisor learned that he had indeed continued to work his other part-time jobs: grading papers for a local class and making his private-practice clinical case notes while on the agency clock.

POOR PERFORMANCE WITH SELF-CARE GOALS MAY LEAD TO POOR JOB PERFORMANCE

I observed that staff members who had difficulty managing/adhering/ attending to their own individualized self-care plans, regardless of their initial enthusiasm, exhibited performance difficulties (regardless of any coaching or corrective activity). These performance difficulties resulted in their being separated from the agency within 6 to 15 months of employment.

I tested my hypothesis by reviewing the personnel files of all staff members who had employment tenure of two years or less. During a 12-year period, I documented the separation of eight employees. We routinely had 19 positions, made up of full-time and part-time employees who were employed in a variety of positions (entry level, program specialist, and leadership). The separated employees

- Encompassed broad levels of experience (3 to 20 years).
- Were diverse racially and ethnically (African American, Latino, and Caucasian).
- Professed a variety of spiritual traditions (Christian, Muslim, pagan, and Catholic).
- Ranged in age from 25 to 65 and included men and women.
- Did not consistently share or have a common supervisor.

What was the common denominator? It was uncanny! They all shared one trait: poor adherence to their self-selected self-care goals.

ADHERENCE TO SELF-CARE GOALS LEADS TO SOLID PERFORMANCE

The evidence that adherence to self-care goals had a positive effect on staff and the agency was proven in a 2012 study.

Increased Self-Care Ratings Show Increased Performance

In the fall of 2012, a former graduate student of mine requested to identify the relationships between individual self-care completion and employee performance as part of her research project thesis/capstone at the University of Colorado Denver School of Public Affairs. (Kawulok, 2012). Kawulok's analysis explored the relationships between individual self-care program success, employee performance, and overall organizational productivity.

To maintain confidentiality, personnel data were extracted by staff members who had legal access to human resource information. The files were redacted and used unique codes assigned to each file. The collected data was obtained from both electronic and paper personnel files. Kawulok matched this data with leave data maintained in a secondary electronic database and not connected to personnel files or annual performance reviews. After the data were collected, CTR provided Kawulok with numerical ratings for individual self-care and annual performance over a six-year period without including employee names or other demographic information.

A mixed-measure research design was used to derive data from 2006 to 2011. Trends in self-care progress were compared with three dependent variables: overall performance, sick leave, and vacation leave. The results produced statistical measures of employee productivity. Correlations between self-care and the overall annual performance review showed a significant, strong linear positive relationship. As self-care ratings increased, so did individual employee overall scores. I had witnessed this evidence, experientially and anecdotally, but it was affirming to have it borne out by objective statistical data. (Kawulok, 2012).

Overall Annual Performance Rating and Self-Care Progress Ratings

In the Kawulok study there was a statistically significant relationship between the self-care ratings and overall annual performance review (APR) scores. (Kawulok, 2012). Based on the data produced by this study, self-care success impacts overall APR scores. (Figure 6.1 shows the annual average for the whole combined staff.)

A Pearson product-moment correlation coefficient was computed to assess the relationships between self-care mean and overall performance rating.

Correlations between the self-care mean and the overall APR scores showed a significant statistical relationship with $\rho = .000$, and Pearson's $r = .851$, showing a strong positive linear relationship. The strong positive linear relationship is indicative that as employee self-care ratings increase, so do employee overall APR scores. This suggests that individuals who are successful in completing their self-care goals will demonstrate overall superior performance when compared to staff who fare poorly on self-care ratings. It is logical to assume that when individuals perform well, the agency experiences organizational benefits, thus supporting the notion that the self-care plan (SCP) at CTR positively influences organizational productivity. In order to demonstrate specific relationships, the presence of causality, and the influence of other variables, it is recommended that a more comprehensive study be performed using an augmented database for statistical analysis.

Additionally, exit interviews from employees who left the agency during the previous five years revealed comparable data. Former employees who resigned or were "managed out" of the agency between 6 and 15 months of employment spoke of their contentment with the salary and benefits (including agency retreats and professional development opportunities). They were unhappy, however, with the agency's level of accountability

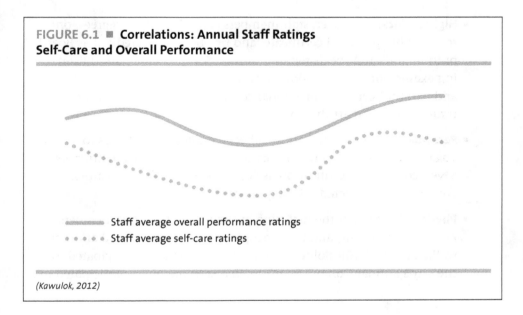

FIGURE 6.1 ■ **Correlations: Annual Staff Ratings Self-Care and Overall Performance**

Staff average overall performance ratings
Staff average self-care ratings

(Kawulok, 2012)

for program performance, including self-care. Many stated they were "frustrated" and in some cases "angry," and alluded to being enmeshed in an unresolved conflict—despite management's efforts to address it. Some had personalized "supervisory comments" about their performance and believed the agency was unyielding. They "didn't like or had problems with" a particular leadership style or a particular policy, and so on. Surprising, at least to me, were statements that they expected nonprofit managers/management to be more laissez-faire.

Although supervisors and directors may be the prompter for the self-care plan, they may become the lightning rod for criticism when they attempt to hold staff accountable for all areas of their job descriptions, and the delicate balance between self-care and performance may go awry.

EVIDENCE OF ACHIEVEMENT FROM STAFF WHO WHOLEHEARTEDLY EMBRACED THE SELF-CARE PROCESS

In contrast to the employees who found fault with their self-designed self-care plans, I have evidenced the staff growth of those who wholeheartedly embraced the process. Over the last 12 years, employees at CTR have stretched, grown, and achieved in a variety of ways, as detailed by the following list of accomplishments *during* their employment.

- **Higher Education:** Seven staff members earned master's degrees, one received her paralegal certificate, and five became accredited as Board of Immigration Appeals representatives. Seven people passed licensing exams—one for juris doctorate; three for clinical social worker and two for licensed professional counselor; and two for level-one trauma-informed art therapy.

- **Personal Growth:** Eight staff members completed 200 hours for Hatha Yoga certification, and three became licensed as Zumba instructors. Seven completed certification as "compassion fatigue educators." One person completed a 10-day silent retreat.

- **Physical Health:** For the first time in their lives, two staff members ran half marathons, and three people ran their first 5K and another walked her first 10K BolderBOULDER. Ten members participated in the city's annual Colfax Marathon. Ten staff members participated in their first six-week boot camp with a personal trainer. Three became vegans/vegetarians. In four "Biggest Loser"-type contests, staff winners lost 38, 53, 16, and 24 pounds.

- **Other Professional and Personal Achievements:** Six staff members presented workshops at national conferences in Alabama, California, Colorado, Florida, Kentucky, Massachusetts, Oregon, and Texas, and one was published in national conference symposium proceedings. Five members completed yearlong leadership institutes designed for people of color. Two staff members became naturalized United States citizens. Three staff members traveled to Panama, England, and Tanzania for 30-day work sabbaticals, and one person traveled to five Latin American countries to participate in Spanish immersion programs (Mexico, Panama, Venezuela, Guatemala, and Costa Rica)!

CONCLUSION

It is thrilling to witness staff blossom! It is gratifying to know that our paradigm change to institutionalize self-care played a role in their achievements. Leadership/management is a necessary component for a staff and an agency to achieve these types of success, as I discuss in the next chapter.

CHAPTER 7

Organizational Barriers to Implementing Individual Self-Care Plans

In the article about the efficacies of strategies for reducing secondary or vicarious trauma published in *Brief Treatment and Crisis Intervention*, Bober and Regehr reported their results from the more than 580 self-reported questionnaires they had sent out to child welfare administrators. (Bober & Regehr, 2006, p. 3). Their research indicated that although administrators typically thought professionally endorsed strategies for decompressing (including self-care) were beneficial, management did not devote time to employing such activities.

In the fall of 2006, I presented our individualized self-care strategy at an annual leadership gathering for executive directors in Winter Park, Colorado. The Institute was a pre-conference event held a day prior to Colorado's statewide conference on domestic violence. I offered our self-care strategy to approximately 35 executive directors as a tool for building morale and increasing staff retention.

In the middle of my presentation, one executive director yelled out,

> *"Are you seriously asking us to do this? I am having heart palpitations just thinking about embarking on such a plan! I barely have enough time to take care of myself. I don't even make it through the month of January with my own New Year's resolutions! And now, you want me to monitor my staff?"*

My response was,

> *"Good point. I agree it is not wise to offer a self-care component if management is not yet ready to embrace it."*

The agency self-care program requires management to be dedicated and fully on board.

PRIMARY REASONS LEADERS ARE RELUCTANT TO ESTABLISH SELF-CARE PROGRAMS

Frankly I was astonished at the level of resistance from professional, educated, seasoned administrators and program supervisors whenever I had the opportunity to present CTR's individualized self-care plan. They blamed their institutions and held tightly to the sentiment that any role they could play would be futile.

After graduation, several of my social work school colleagues secured positions with the Denver Department of Human Services (DDHS) in 2002. Within a few years, they were bemoaning their career choice and some had received "medical prescriptions" for stress leave. In 2012, DDHS management offered child-protection workers an opportunity to address vicarious trauma. They contracted with us to provide our Health Enabling for Listening Professionals (HELP) workshop. Many employees lamented that they were "infected" and it was "too little, too late." Initially, they were pessimistic, believing that nothing short of resigning employment with the agency would be helpful. (CTR HELP Workshops, 2013, Group communication). We allowed them to vent and validated their feelings. We encouraged them to participate in our resilience-building activities and create customized self-care plans with accountability partners. And, we advocated with the DDHS to continue to support employees suffering from compassion fatigue. At the end of the day, the employees welcomed our approach and the ability to gain more control over their lives.

In my quest to encourage local nonprofit executive directors to consider establishing a self-care program for their nonprofit agency, several shared with me the primary reasons that they were reluctant to do so.

Reason 1: *"I don't want too much personal information about my staff."*

Some directors believed that knowing the self-care intentions of their staff would actually interfere with their supervision. They questioned:

- "What if I start to have too much sympathy for a situation and then I am unable to hold my staff accountable?"
- "What if I become envious of a staff member's progress?"
- "What if they want personal disclosures from me?"

I suggested to my colleagues that a level of empathy is always indicated, and having more information potentially opens up additional avenues to address concerns or prod productivity. Professional boundaries, if established at the onset, should remain intact.

Reason 2: *"I don't think it is my job."*

Some executives questioned if the role of "life coach" was part of their position.

- "Quite frankly, and while I wouldn't say this publicly, I just don't care that much."
- "I don't think it is my job. I would rather spend my time cultivating new donors, fundraising, or recruiting board members."
- "I am keeping them employed . . . so doesn't that qualify as a type of self-care?"

Channeling energy in an efficient manner and sustaining the organization are priorities for any executive. I shared with my colleagues examples of the positive impact that a high-functioning, high-morale workplace can have on fundraising. Staff members are more willing to assist in advertising nonprofit events to their family and friends. I pointed out that staff members can offer immense untapped resources in order to gain board members, donors, and program ingenuity. Is there ever enough time or money? Should that always be our excuse?

Reason 3: *"Staying employed in the nonprofit sector is its own intrinsic reward."*

Some executives are convinced that compassion fatigue—and the resultant badge of honor—are part of the payoff for nonprofit work.

- "I am already fighting the good fight and doing the good work."
- "Every nonprofit is in the same boat—we have to do more with less."
- "Well, it could be worse—I could be working for a corporation."

An occasional award or local recognition for their tirelessness and sacrifice are "as good as it gets." I asked them to ponder the gains of having more energy. I dared them to change their perception and erase the standard that working for a nonprofit meant giving up any quality of life.

Reason 4: *"I just don't believe in it."*

A few executives resisted the whole idea and didn't see any merit in the program.

- "Our workload, staff reductions, and time-sensitive projects make regular self-care next to impossible."
- "It is just another thing to add to our mile-long list and another disappointment when it doesn't get done."
- "Self-care, shmelf-care—it doesn't really make a difference, it's just the latest trend."

A minority of executives expressed cynicism and resentment and they could only think of the downside. When this was the case, I submitted that until they or their program "crashed and burned" not much would change at their agency.

Reason 5: *"I don't want to be the model."*

Executives who voiced this reason were apprehensive about feeling exposed, especially with their staff. To undertake a self-care program would mean "getting it together and keeping it together." Some executives smirked and said,

- "As long as we have the mantle of the overworked, overwrought, underappreciated executive, all of our deficits are more likely to be understood, overlooked, and excused."

- "I feel scrutinized (by my board) already and this would put me in the spotlight!"

- "It would be too much of a struggle for me; I don't have the energy."

I am perplexed by these statements. I usually reiterate that (as an executive myself) I understand that the prospect of implementing yet another program is not always a welcomed task. Yet, in my experience, I believe—and *I know*—in order to stay relevant, attending to emerging issues and promising practices will keep an agency vibrant.

CONCLUSION

A leader doesn't have to be perfect, just a lifelong learner, looking forward. It appears that too often, we are the ones getting in our own way.

CHAPTER 8

Modeling the Self-Care Concept

Now we come to the most difficult and scary part of developing a self-care plan for your agency. The plan begins with a committed executive and expands to the agency leadership team. As the executive director, you are the *model*—a small replica of the real thing!

Embarking on and sustaining a self-care plan is a substantial leadership undertaking. Undoubtedly a critical component of the plan is how leadership personnel model for the rest of the agency. A frazzled, easily annoyed, overwhelmed, disorganized, and chronically complaining supervisor who routinely exhibits poor eating, poor exercise habits, and a disheveled or poorly put-together appearance by taking "business casual" to an extreme (yes, grooming has a role here!) sends a message of incongruence and may negatively (even if subliminally) impact the integrity of the plan.

I will be the first to say that I have not always been a shining example of the individualized self-care plan. It became important to heed the message. One year, after an incredibly intense year of work, a staff member posted a comedic note on my desk phone that said, *"If you lived here, you would be home by now."*

Unwittingly, every February I began to feel annoyed and aggrieved. Why did everyone else leave at the stroke of 5:00 p.m.? Why was I in the office until 7:00, or on some evenings until 10:00? Why did I have to stay ahead of the curve while others were okay with being prodded? Why did I have to sacrifice my gym, dance, dinner dates, and so on, and find myself reviewing journal articles, searching for documents, organizing common areas, making endless to-do lists, and attending to the little things that made our environment warm and inviting?

Why was I the only person at work on Saturday or Sunday (or both) and telling myself that I preferred it, that it was quiet and I could get more work accomplished? I rationalized that I would feel great on Monday morning. For a while it worked. I did feel great, but the high did not last. I became uncharacteristically cranky and reclusive, and I realized I resented over-functioning and putting in all of those hours.

SELF-CARE AND THE EXECUTIVE DIRECTOR

The nonprofit organizational infrastructure commonly suggests that the board of directors is the entity responsible for evaluating the executive director. In my experience—both being on a board and being supervised by board members—I know that boards offer support and a listening ear, but due to time limitations, they may not be able to offer ongoing mentoring or coaching. An engaged board, however, has many options, one being to develop a personnel committee that would provide a regular review of the executive director's self-care plan.

Each year after I create my self-care plan, I invite a few friends and/or colleagues to become my support circle. Although I am internally driven and acutely aware of secondary trauma, I am deeply aware that I must stay attuned or I will not be able to continue to effectively work in the trauma sector. It has been exceptionally helpful to converse with *my own* group of colleagues or friends who "keep me honest" by telling me the truth and holding me accountable to my self-care goals.

On occasion, circle members professed that they wanted to adopt a plan of their own. We created a monthly coffee check-in that allows venting, along with gathering support from each other. We incentivized our efforts so that our plans would be a little more competitive. One year we each agreed to contribute a $200 gift card to the person who accomplished the majority of his or her goals.

The "Year of No"

In 2007, my intellectual self-care goal was to begin a "Year of No." The previous two years had been arduous for me personally and professionally. My mother's health became critical, and my agency had merged two programs from a dissolved nonprofit: a legal immigration and social enterprise program that included three new staff members (two of whom were troublesome and obstinate). And, I was teaching a part-time class for a local university. I had burned the proverbial candle at both ends and was exhausted. I decided that—for an entire year—I would not add anything to my professional plate. For a whole year, I said, "I am sorry. I am not able to assist with or commit to, or be present for, anything else this year." I declined invitations, stating, "It's my year of 'no.'" People were incredulous. "Your year of what? You must be joking!" "My career would be over, I could never do that!" Frankly, I was amazed and amused at the responses. It was telling. So many leaders believed that their work lives were out of their control. Undoubtedly, I missed out on a couple of "once-in-a-lifetime" opportunities, but at year-end, I felt invigorated and proud of myself!

A STARTING POINT

Executives can begin by designing their own self-care plan and finding peers who act as both a support and accountability group. Allow several months or a year practicing this phase of the wellness program prior to offering it to others. A practice period will give leadership an idea of what *stretch goals* involve, as well as how it feels to be accountable for them. It will take time to process and practice this new concept.

Establish and Maintain Personal Boundaries

Establish and maintain boundaries for yourself in the workplace as an essential opportunity to model wellness and self-care. Practice what you will soon be teaching. Begin by adhering to a traditional 40-hour week. Cease checking (and responding to) emails night and day. Take lunch breaks away from your desk. Stay home if you are not feeling well instead of moping around and risking spreading germs. Keep vacations sacred. Of course, there will be time-sensitive exceptions; make them the exceptions and not the rule.

As you may recall, I spent several years in my African-American peer support group listening, talking, and sharing. I must admit, at times, being a crusader for self-care felt selfish. That is the first hurdle that you (and your peers) may wish to address. Why are we spending this time on ourselves when we could be taking care of someone or something else? Years later I read these words from author Toni Cade Bambara:

> *Revolution begins with the self, in the self. It may be lonely. Certainly painful. It'll take time. We've got time. That of course is an unpopular utterance these days. We'd better take the time to fashion revolutionary selves, revolutionary lives, revolutionary relationships. If your house ain't in order, you ain't in order. It is so much easier to be out there than right here. The revolution ain't out there. Yet. But it is here.* (Bambara, 1970, pp. 133–135).

Consider Recruiting a Mentor or Consultant to Coach You Through Your "Practice" Year

It will take time to wholly integrate this new concept. Executives may consider recruiting a mentor or consultant to act as the goad for their practice year. Think about people whom you admire, who are disciplined, organized, and productive. They may not work in your industry and yet can cheerlead for your new investment in yourself. Also, there are a variety of self-care books, DVDs, and online coaches (if you prefer the electronic method). Be honest! If you are having trouble adhering to your plan, share your hindrances instead of minimizing or masking them. I prefer face-to-face interactions with coaches/consultants who will keep me honest and help me avoid the temptation to rationalize my behavior.

Establish and Maintain Organizational Boundaries

Engaged executives take pride in being open, flexible, thoughtful, and imaginative about staying on course with their mission and getting community needs met. Nevertheless, the ability to say "no" is a valuable skill to learn and practice internally and externally with the philanthropic community.

Continuing to "do more with less" is a hallmark of nonprofit work. We feel so fortunate to get any portion of our proposed grant that we neglect to revise the goals and objectives when the award is reduced by 10 to 50 percent. Instead of overworking and overburdening staff in an attempt to realize the original goals . . . revise them. Inform the funder which objectives can be met with their awarded funds. Is it a risk to do so? Potentially. However, after analyzing the cost of the project and speaking with the funder, in 97 percent of the cases the funder concurred. Of the 3 percent of funders that disagreed, one had requested to "see the clients" attending our children's support groups; another wanted us to alter our operations to meet the funder's political agenda, and the last percent refused to fund a component of our program they deemed was "too cutting edge." Our agency declined all requests and lost their funding. It's really six of one or half-a-dozen of another. Continuing to do more with less has a cost.

The unequivocal "no" response from leadership is not always well received by employees. The "no" may refer to a variety of situations:

- "No, you may not take off every Friday before a holiday weekend."

- "No, you may not continue to miss deadlines without a consequence."

- "No, you may not use the volunteer/intern program as a personal dating service."

- "No, you may not use agency accounts for your personal business."

- "No you may not use rude, harsh language in email correspondence."

People who work closely together on intense or social justice issues usually share passions and philosophies. They tend to stay connected via social media and spend time together outside of the office. They confide in each other, socialize, and may attend the same cultural and community events.

Friendships blossom and mutual interests find a home in the workplace. I do not condone any attempt of management to legislate or legitimize relationships; however, I have found policy guidance in this area to be helpful in identifying potential conflicts of interests. Social media instruments (Facebook, Instagram, Twitter, YouTube, blogging, etc.) can both create and destroy.

If a leader desires an agency that values lifelong learning and the cultivation of an inspired staff, he or she should be mindful of employees' emerging relationships and provide space for discussions on boundaries.

Staff members may incorrectly assume that the nonprofit organization has an ownership role in the maintenance of their personal relationships.

Real-Life EXAMPLE

Several years ago an employee became ill and underwent a serious surgery. Victoria lived alone and did not have any family in the state. Per usual, management circulated a get-well card and sent flowers or fruit to her. Several staff members, including members of leadership, visited the employee at the hospital.

A week or so later, during a staff meeting, one of Victoria's colleagues lashed out at me, "You need to help her! She needs someone to get her prescriptions filled, pick up her mail, park her car in a safer location, et cetera." I was stunned and responded that I personally (indeed leadership) did not have a responsibility to do these things; however, I fully supported any of her friends on staff to coordinate these tasks for her.

On occasion, employees brood, sulk, and complain. Some exhibit distress publicly and seek to entangle others in their misfortune. Disgruntled staff may begin to build a case against you or the organization about any slight, any error you have ever made, and speak in inflammatory language. Angry comments aimed at me over the years include:

- "This agency is a sham."
- "This disciplinary action is a witch hunt!"
- "You are unfriendly and uncaring."
- "I would have stayed with the agency longer except I couldn't work with you!"
- "You are a disappointment to women of color. When did you die?"

When I am not too tired or disappointed by these outbursts, I try to understand. We ask our clients to trust us and share themselves with us. We see our clients at their most vulnerable, weak, destroyed selves . . . and we empathize. We want to be good, do well, and be the hero who saves them. We believe that we are "the ones who know best" and anyone and anything that interferes with personal advocacy or mission becomes the enemy—hence, management.

At the end of the day, we can't practice well unless we stay well.

CONCLUSION

Instituting boundaries may be unpopular with staff. Yet doing so is necessary for leadership to create and maintain a healthy environment. Just as setting and maintaining perimeters around emotional health is important, so too are those perimeters around financial health, as the next chapter illustrates.

them. We believe that we [illegible] best" and anyone and anything that interferes with personal [illegible] itself becomes the enemy—hence, [illegible] management.

At the end of [illegible] we can't [illegible] we stay well.

CONCLUSION

Introducing boundaries [illegible] appropriate [illegible] is [illegible] necessary for leadership [illegible] maintain [illegible] environments. Just as setting and maintaining appropriate [illegible] and [illegible] is [illegible] important, so too are these [illegible] as the [illegible] chapter illustrates.

CHAPTER 9

Funding for Self-Care in Nonprofit Organizations

What are the costs and savings—financial and emotional—that an agency incurs and gains with the creation and implementation of a self-care program? For most leaders cost is their number-one concern. However, nonprofit executives are always amazed when I share how self-care plans not only positively affect employee performance, but the bottom line.

HOW MUCH DOES IT COST?

The prevailing questions on every director's mind are:

- How much does it cost?
- Do you have self-care as a line item in the agency's budget?
- Is the workweek abbreviated so that staff can attend to their self-care goals?

My answer is absolute: "It depends."

I wish I could share with you the recipe and give you a sample budget. The truth is that there is no recipe! The investment in employee self-care and a wellness-focused agency is complex and requires thought, creativity, and intention.

On the whole, individualized self-care plans do not cost an agency a dime. How can that be? Staff members create plans based on their desire to be a more integrated, balanced person. They purposely center on themselves and their life outside of the agency.

In my experience, the *majority* of staff members do not hold an expectation that the agency is liable for their selection or success (as shown in the examples for each category) with a particular goal. In fact, the *majority* of staff stretch goals have very little to do with agency work.

The lack of funding for "training on self-care" has been cited as a barrier to implementing self-care plans. (Busch-Armendariz, Kalergis, & Garza, 2009, p. 1). Yet many agencies have a budget line item for "continuing education or professional development," and each staff member may be allotted varying amounts to attend to this goal. In fact, expenditures for individual self-care activities may align with existing agency goals. If a goal is congruent with agency or program objectives, leadership may make these funds available if the supervisee has a self-care goal that also enhances agency performance.

Real-Life EXAMPLE

One of our receptionists, Darlene, listed as her intellectual goal "to enroll in a once-a-week, year-long Spanish class." She desired to become a bilingual person. She requested to use a portion of her professional development funds to pay for the class. She reasoned that she would be more prepared to welcome and better assist Spanish-speaking clients and visitors. Darlene's request was honored.

Real-Life EXAMPLE

Karina wanted to learn the basics of American Sign Language (ASL) as part of her self-care and intellectual development goal. Serendipitously, the agency had been asked to supervise a deaf/hearing-impaired intern. Karina agreed to supervise the intern. An ASL class was offered on a Monday, one hour before the end of the workday. Karina requested that her supervisor allow her to "use work hours" to take the class and said she would agree to pay for the class. Her request was honored.

I believe "leadership paralysis" may be a more accurate description than financial deficiencies. In fact, implementing a self-care program can be as simple as flexible schedules—so staff can exercise or take part in nourishing activities, *consistent* supervision, peer coaching/debriefing, potlucks and recognizing staff members with celebrations, tours/retreats, accessing the abundance of library or Internet wellness video resources for training, book/video discussions, and capitalizing on the artistic interests or expertise of employees or community members eager to share or donate.

- Julia shared her interest in aromatherapy, and one afternoon the staff made eye pillows.
- Kevin shared his interest in music therapy and hosted a staff singalong.
- Kathi shared her skill in creating personalized journals and assisted staff in creating their own.

Of course, any self-care program may be lobbied with the declaration "I want the agency to purchase xyz (massages, an espresso machine, etc.) or permit xyz (two-hour lunch breaks, on-site day care, etc.) because it will make me a happier, more contented employee!" These exclamations may require a review of the role and function of individualized self-care plans.

Once, while shopping, I overheard a woman try to convince her spouse to purchase more running outfits: "Honey, I need to buy more (expensive) attractive running outfits. If I look good, I will feel good, and if I feel good, I will run more, and if I run more you'll get the benefits at home!" I almost burst out laughing. But, this is exactly the logic that leadership may hear from employees. Nonprofits are stewards of public funds. We must earn and maintain this trust.

There is no room for frivolous frittering of funds. If the staff member's request is reasonable and equitable, I would support using allotted staff development funds to grant the request.

HOW MUCH DOES IT SAVE?

Remarkably, I am rarely asked, "How much money does a self-care plan save an organization?" There are a number of cost-saving measures that are correlated with individual self-care plans:

- Payroll leave expenses
- Workers' compensation
- Health insurance
- Advertising, recruitment, and training

Payroll Leave Expenses

Historically, our expenses have been minimal as they relate to sick and disability time. Staff members (full-time equivalent) earn 96 hours of sick leave annually, which can be used to care for ill family members. In fact, staff had accumulated so much sick leave, the board (at the suggestion of our human resource attorney) approved the creation of an Extended Sick Leave Bank. Employees who had earned more than six weeks of leave were paid a portion of their remaining hours. Future sick leave earnings have been capped at six weeks or 240 hours for full-time employees.

Workers' Compensation

CTR benefits from our state workers' compensation program, which offers discounted premiums as an incentive for having a safety program on-site. In 2013, the agency was awarded a Safety of Circle award from Pinnacol Assurance for "exceptional performance in safety, loss prevention, financial and claims management." And, they catered lunch for the entire staff!

Health Insurance

As the country's insurance costs soared, we met with an independent health broker. He informed us that we were paying high rates for claims because of the agency's membership in an association with a "notoriously unhealthy cross-section" of the nonprofit sector. For many years, we had been enrolled with other Colorado nonprofits in this association's health insurance plan, believing that a "nonprofit association group rate" was saving us money. Armed with this information, we decided to break from the association. Our broker identified a variety of premiums/plans for our small group.

Our staff members ranged from 25 to 65 years of age, all were nonsmokers, and most were physically active. Leadership requested new underwriting. We saved 30 percent on health premiums during our first year! Three years later, in 2011, when insurance premiums were rising 12 percent in Colorado, our healthcare broker stunned us by stating that our healthcare cost had actually dropped 8 percent!

Advertising, Recruitment, and Training

Research confirms that when businesses take care of their workers, they are better able to retain them. (Employment Policy Foundation, 2002; *Protecting employees, employers and the public*, 2009). The agency was established in 1987 and implemented its self-care program in 2002. On average, CTR has a total of 19 employees. During the period 2002–2014, six staff members in leadership or program specialist positions had remained employed for 15-plus years and four others for more than eight years. The average length of employment for mid-level professional staff was five years and for leadership was 10 years—a rarity for the nonprofit trauma field, which has mind-boggling staff attrition. Our entry-level positions, including front office/receptionist and frontline entry-level (undergraduate) crisis counselor, are stepping-stone positions that turn over every two to three years. These employees are usually new undergraduates and are beginning their careers.

Advertising, recruiting, screening résumés, interviewing candidates, ordering and reviewing Colorado Bureau of Investigation reports, and checking references, along with the new-hire orientation process, are not only time-consuming tasks but require acuity and wholehearted investment. As Jim Collins (2001) said, "Getting the right people on the bus" is no small investment of energy. (Collins, 2001; Collins, 2005, p. 2). We have enjoyed one of the lowest staff attrition rates in Colorado compared to mission-similar nonprofits in the state.

Have we made poor hiring decisions? Absolutely. Have we coached, mentored, guided, and been cheerleaders for too long, tolerating argumentative, sullen, negative, and discourteous employees? Absolutely. Have we been the target of irate and slanderous emails and letters from disgruntled ex-employees? Yep. Have we separated and *encouraged* resignations from poorly suited employees, sometimes in cohorts of three staff members in a year? Affirmative. The individualized self-care plan is not a cure-all for what ails an agency. Yet, it supports our staff mission of *"promoting accountability, trust and respect . . . ."* We have stayed the course, believing the benefits continue to exceed the challenges.

CONCLUSION

Fundraising is a never-ending endeavor for nonprofit executives. The return on our investment is ensured when employee self-care is a consideration.

CHAPTER 10

Beyond the Anecdotes— Establishing a Health-Promoting Environment

In "Strategies for Reducing Secondary or Vicarious Trauma: Do They Work?" Bober and Regehr report that organizational attempts at self-care and supervision lack validity, and they call for a structural solution instead of an individual one. They call for workplaces that can prevent, identify, or reduce vicarious trauma and declare that it is urgently needed. (Bober & Regehr, 2006).

I agree. The individual self-care plan is likely to be unsuccessful if it is the *only* component of an agency well-being initiative. It will falter and likely fail if it is not supported by other health-protection policies and practices. Tom Rath and Jim Harter, authors of *Wellbeing: The Five Essential Elements*, discuss distinct areas of employee engagement, which include career, social, financial, physical, and community. (Rath & Harter, 2010). The practice of self-care needs to be fully integrated into the heart and fabric of the agency.

As I have shared in previous chapters, a tokenism approach is not sustainable or successful in an attempt to develop a more racially, culturally diverse and inclusive workplace. Likewise, the literature, along with my experience, suggests that if individualized self-care is isolated from other health-promoting practices, the idea of self-care is just that, only an idea. Our prototype offers new hope for recruiting, retaining, sustaining, and growing professionals who can extend the reach of your mission and positively affect your bottom line!

The following 10 health-protection principles practiced by our organization advance the philosophy of self-care and agency wellness. We capitalized on several principles to attract new clients, businesses, and funders. Albeit there is no right path or single best approach, any effort to design and institutionalize agency well-being must be customized to your environment. I believe the plan should be visionary, flexible, congruent, and inform *all* decision-making, no matter how minute. At its core, a wellness practice is inclusive, participatory, and will likely sustain itself.

CTR's individualized self-care plan has been celebrated, highlighted, and publicized as our attempt to cope with the complex task of dealing with secondary and vicarious trauma. In 2010, we were thrilled to win First Place in the Carson J Spencer Foundation's *Working Minds Contest—Celebrating Mentally Healthy Workplaces in Colorado*. I credit the successes of our program to the development of health protection principles—accepting challenges, being proactive instead of reactive, and understanding that leadership, agency infrastructure, and culture share responsibility for employee well-being.

CREATING A WELLNESS PROGRAM AT YOUR AGENCY—10 PRINCIPLES

On our journey, I discovered 10 principles that I believe contribute to the success of our individualized self-care plans, resulting in the creation of an invigorated agency and energized staff.

- **Principle 1:** Begin with the Job Description (and Not the Salary!)

- **Principle 2:** Invest in a Generous Benefits Package

- **Principle 3:** Create Staff Mission and Inclusiveness Philosophy Statements

- **Principle 4:** Attend to Agency Inclusiveness and Recognition of Historical Trauma (a.k.a. Historical Unresolved Grief)

- **Principle 5:** Offer Clinical and Program Supervision

- **Principle 6:** Design Conflict Resolution Policies and Establish Boundaries

- **Principle 7:** Ensure the Agency Provides a Safe Environment—Physically and Psychologically

- **Principle 8:** Formalize Staff Involvement (a.k.a. Team Building)

- **Principle 9:** Require Continuing Education (a.k.a. Staff Training)

- **Principle 10:** Redesign the Annual Employee Review

Consider these principles, which I discuss in the following subsections, as a set of guidelines to help you establish an infrastructure in which your individualized self-care plan can thrive. Of course, depending on your current structure, you may want to tweak, add, or completely overhaul your current systems. Don't take my word for it—survey staff, stakeholders, donors, and clients. Get an objective and current reading on how things are going.

PRINCIPLE 1: BEGIN WITH THE JOB DESCRIPTION (AND NOT THE SALARY!)

Review agency job descriptions. Do they align with a philosophy of self-care? Why have I designated this item as number one? To answer this question, I encourage you to scan job postings for local nonprofit positions.

Job Descriptions Should Be Reasonable

Many cities have nonprofit membership associations and typically post recruitment and job opportunities. The job descriptions often read like two or even three positions rolled into one as in the example in Figure 10.1, which was listed on the Colorado Nonprofit Association's job bank in Denver, Colorado.

The lengthy list of qualifications would give any candidate pause, especially with terms such as "natural ability." Is there such a thing? How do you prove that you have positive relationships with youth?

Job descriptions should be reasonable. Certainly positions may have both primary and secondary responsibilities. However, the position should not become a dumping ground for everything you would like for the position

FIGURE 10.1 ■ Sample Violence Prevention Coordinator Job Description

VIOLENCE PREVENTION COORDINATOR

The Violence Prevention Coordinator's primary responsibility is to coordinate the day-to-day operations of dating violence prevention programs. The Coordinator is a direct service position that leads prevention educators, volunteers, and interns in program implementation and manages program growth, marketing, and evaluation. The Coordinator actively develops and maintains relationships with schools and community agencies. Additionally, the Coordinator advises and facilitates activities for all sponsored student clubs.

JOB FUNCTIONS/RESPONSIBILITIES

1. Coordinate the activities, marketing, and growth of prevention programs.
2. Direct the day-to-day activities of other prevention staff.
3. Assist and/or lead the selection, orientation, and training of prevention staff.
4. Advise and facilitate activities for sponsored student clubs in collaboration with faculty sponsors and other staff (where applicable).
5. Facilitate prevention programs throughout the city (teaching HR classes to students in middle and high schools, leading gender-specific psycho-educational groups, and coordinating school-wide prevention education).
6. Offer appropriate support, referral information, and crisis intervention services as needed for individual youth identified through prevention programs.
7. Provide professional trainings and community outreach on related topics.
8. Coordinate the collection of program evaluation data, including pre/post surveys, individual and group encounters, presentation statistics, and program participant data.
9. Establish and maintain relationships with schools and other agencies who use prevention programs.
10. Direct and organize the scheduling of prevention programs.
11. Initiate and monitor school invoicing for prevention programs.
12. Maintain and order prevention program supplies.
13. Lead regular team meetings with all prevention staff and the Program Director.
14. Consult regularly with the Program Director regarding the day-to-day operations of prevention programs, successes and challenges, and other job responsibilities.
15. Assist the Program Director in monitoring prevention program data to ensure grant and contract compliance.
16. Assist the Program Director as needed in grant reporting and preparation related to the prevention programs.

17. Educate the community about prevention programs by serving on at least one community taskforce or committee and by assisting the Program Director in maintaining existing community relationships and pursuing new community partners.
18. Engage in professional development through attending workshops and trainings and participating in community-level networking meetings.
19. Attend all-staff trainings and other all-staff meetings as deemed appropriate by the Program Director.
20. Other duties as assigned by the Program Director.

EDUCATION

- Master's in a human service field (bachelor's considered with minimum 4 years)

EXPERIENCE

- Minimum 3 years direct service experience with youth in schools and/or community settings
- Leadership and implementation of prevention education programming
- Classroom presentation and public speaking with demonstrated success
- Training, mentoring, and directing staff and volunteers
- Aptitudes/Abilities: Awareness and sensitivity to cultural, ethnic, and socioeconomic differences
- In-depth knowledge of teen dating violence, domestic violence, and child abuse
- Proven ability to establish positive relationships with groups of youth
- Self-motivation and ability to motivate others
- Comfort with organizing multiple and varied responsibilities
- Natural ability to work collaboratively with other agencies, schools, and community groups
- Desire to develop and implement new programs
- Strong verbal and written communication skills
- Computer proficiency (including social networking) and ability to quickly learn new systems
- Leadership of people (especially youth) from diverse perspectives and backgrounds
- Ability to work well in team environment

to accomplish but cannot get funded. Analyze the components of a job description and ask yourself if you would respond to the advertisement or accept it.

Real-Life EXAMPLE

I supervised a young woman (with permission from her executive director) who was employed as the director of advocacy for another crisis-intervention agency. According to her director, as one of two people of color in the agency, she did not feel understood by supervisors. Cheryl was on call for *three* programs within the agency! She was the crisis backup for the general (English) hotline, crisis backup for the Spanish-speaking hotline, and administrative backup for the agency case managers. I know, because she was interrupted by several calls during one of our supervisions. She nonchalantly stated, "Because I am bilingual, it is part of my job description to always be on call." Professionally, I thought it was an administrative error in judgment. I suggested that I speak to her director. Before I could schedule time to speak to the executive director of her agency, Cheryl resigned. She had remained in her position for less than a year.

In 2009, three years later, I hired a young woman who had worked for the above-mentioned organization. She confirmed that she carried the on-call phone for the Spanish-speaking hotline 24 hours a day, seven days a week, for eight months! In fact, the agency's Spanish hotline calls were transferred to her personal cell phone!

Cross-train Staff and Capitalize on Their Skills and Experience

Nonprofits should capitalize on the skills and experience of candidates who offer more than the technical elements of a job description. Cross-training develops bench strength for all workers in every position. At CTR, the director of training and volunteer services (DTVS) is a licensed professional counselor. She is responsible for recruiting staff and interns/volunteers, interviewing, training, and hosting recognition ceremonies.

She prepares these individuals to work on our hotline (or special events). After completing their training, she transfers their supervision to the director of the hotline (DHS).

The two directors work together on hotline staffing, continuing education, and supervision issues. If there is a concern about training, the DTVS handles it. If there is a concern about staffing the hotline, the DHS manages the matter. The DTVS uses her licensed professional counselor skills and knowledge about crisis/trauma. She can assist with clinical concerns encountered by volunteers/interns and provide "intern field supervision" including, on occasion, the co-facilitation of counseling sessions. However, crisis counseling is not part of her job description.

Our DHS is responsible for operations of the 24-hour hotline and any program staff while they respond to our hotline callers. If questions on scheduling or other hotline protocols arise once agency training (for staff or volunteers) has been completed, the DTVS is out of the loop and the DHS is the point person. The DHS complements the DTVS, assisting with our biannual volunteer training, and on occasion may interview potential interns. The DHS gives input on emerging issues and makes requests for educational topics or additional training—but she is not the point person for its implementation.

In fact, agencywide, all administrative support staff members are trained to respond to crisis calls and connect clients to the appropriate staff person in the agency. Although they may not be skilled in crisis intervention, they can offer courteous emotional support while getting callers connected to a counselor. In addition, all management staff occasionally make coffee for clients, answer phones, offer trainings, shop for office supplies, produce their own correspondence, take out their own trash, and troubleshoot simple computer issues.

The Leadership Team has a written policy on internal operations (see Figure 10.2). Our model describes how we honor our responsibilities to each other. In fact, we have a Leadership Guide for the following leadership/management positions and departments:

- Administration
- Building Policies

- Front Office Operations

- Fundraising/Special Events

- Elder Program

- Children's Program

- Mi Gente–VAWA Legal Solutions

- Hotline Program

- Volunteer/Intern Program

- Finance

- Befriending the Body—Trauma-Sensitive Yoga

- Inclusiveness Orientation

- The Translation & Interpreting Center

Each guide details how to be successful in the implementation of a particular program. New hires do not start from scratch!

Promote an Inclusive Philosophy with Job Descriptions

Every job description and our inclusive philosophy are intended to both "find and grow" people. Staff may be hired with a degree or *equivalent experience*, and bilingual (Spanish) skill is preferred *for all positions* in the agency (not only reception and outreach staff). Talented people, particularly people of color, are not screened out because they had not been fortunate enough to get a college or graduate degree.

Real-Life EXAMPLE

Several years ago, we hired a woman in her mid-thirties. Juanita had the required equivalent work experience, but not a college degree (due to a lack of financial support and a history of domestic violence, addiction, and prostitution). Three years after she was employed with CTR, she asked the organization to support/sponsor her application for an education scholarship designed for domestic violence survivors. Juanita completed her undergraduate education as a dean's list scholar and remained with CTR for eight years!

FIGURE 10.2 ■ **Leadership Team Policy on Internal Operations**

The Center for Trauma & Resilience
Leadership Team Overview

GOAL: To create a leadership team whose members will provide vision, agency oversight and accountability for all program and administrative areas.

TEAM GUIDELINES

1. Each team member will have primary responsibility over her/his program area.

2. No member will make a decision with regard to a matter for which she/he does not have primary responsibility. Issues that arise in another area of responsibility should be referred back to the appropriate program.

3. Team members will bring concerns, ideas, criticisms, etc., to team meetings for discussion, and refrain from expressing public criticism of a team leader or program's work.

4. The Executive Director will be the team leader. Decisions will be made after all team members have expressed their opinions, concerns and ideas. Caveat: the final authority to make decisions lies with the Executive Director.

5. Within each program each team member is expected to make decisions. However, certain decisions will be made with input from the team, including:

   - adding/deleting services
   - financial appropriations
   - policy changes

6. Each team member makes a commitment to keep the leadership team informed about her/his actions and activities. Effective communication allows each program to operate with the maximum of autonomy.

7. Some issues will arise where responsibility is unclear. It is each team member's responsibility to help identify gray areas and bring the issue to the team for discussion.

©The Center for Trauma & Resilience

I have a resignation letter (still) posted above my desk from a young Latina who worked at our agency for 15 months. Her letter states that I, as the director, was responsible for her short tenure. She says my continued emphasis on higher education and people of color sparked her decision to apply for graduate school earlier than she anticipated. She completed her master's in public health and later enrolled in the Peace Corps.

PRINCIPLE 2: INVEST IN A GENEROUS BENEFITS PACKAGE

Employment aficionados agree that a competitive salary is a major draw for a position. Is there more your agency can offer? I have never forgotten my mother's advice to "always accept the position with the best benefits package!"

Human resource studies clearly demonstrate that the costs incurred by losing employees (advertising, interviewing, orienting, and training a replacement) are often far greater than the cost of providing adequate benefits and leave for current employees. The average cost of turnover is 20 percent of an employee's total annual compensation (Boushey & Glynn, 2012).

In our trauma-serving agency, the provision of 100 percent employer-paid medical, dental, and vision benefits is just the beginning. We have been able to maintain this standard through all the ups and downs of the health insurance industry. Staff members pay for coverage for partners or children, but we have proudly and happily provided agency-paid coverage for full-time employees.

Is there more? Yes, everyone begins with three weeks of vacation (which expands with tenure to four and five weeks) and 12 days of sick leave, which are accrued as eight hours per month. Sick leave may be used to care for children or elderly/disabled parents.

An employee who is visibly ill or states that he or she is not feeling well is *required* to go home. To further support optimal health, staff members work an eight-hour day with a one-hour paid lunch break. Staff members are encouraged to leave their desks in order to enjoy their lunch and to discourage "working lunches."

If employees have regular intervals of time off from work, there will be less "I" trouble—as described by one staff member as the "I just can't see coming to work today!" phenomenon. At the staff initiation, we offer a vacation donor plan. An employee can donate vacation hours to another person (sick leave is not included) for any reason, at any time.

Staff may not be contacted for *any reason* while they are taking sick or vacation leave.

Employees can participate in supplemental insurance plans, including tax-exempt 403(b) savings plans. And, although we do not have the mandated number of employees, our policies honor the spirit of the federal Family Medical Leave Act (FMLA). And, we provide insurance for employees (and volunteers) through an Accidental Death and Dismemberment policy.

We recognize 11 holidays a year. We observe (in conjunction with our inclusiveness philosophy) Martin Luther King Jr. Day, Cesar Chavez Day, the first day of Kwanzaa, and a floating personal day for everyone including observers of Ramadan, Hanukkah, etc.

Other benefits include biweekly clinical supervision for clinical staff, provided by a licensed consultant on contract with the agency. In addition, the agency pays the annual required state regulatory database fee for staff to be listed as mental health counselors.

We offer flexible work schedules, to ensure staff members adhere to an eight-hour workday. If staff members work during an early morning, evening, or weekend event, they "flex" their schedules to compensate (during the same week or pay period). There is no formal accumulation of "comp" time, which curtails its byproducts "burnout and fatigue" and the amassing of hours and hours of time that members are unable to take. Telecommuting provisions are available for staff who may, on rare occasions, need to work off-site. Staff flextime includes the ability to attend personal or family events such as soccer championship games, dance/music/theater recitals, or graduations.

One of my greatest achievements is the reward of a 30-day, 50 percent paid sabbatical for employees who have accrued five years of continuous employment. Staff members have traveled to Tanzania, Panama, and London, and returned energized and enthusiastic.

It is not unusual for nonprofits to experience lean economic years. These years require leadership to get creative. Small one-time merit awards (for example, extra time off, parking on-site) are possible ways to reward staff. Pre-holiday breakfast or lunch celebrations—such as grilling/cookouts with music and lighthearted conversation—and/or early departures from work on the eve of major holidays make a positive impression.

Occasionally, I have dipped into my own pocket and catered lunch (my famous vegetarian chili), secured leadership education opportunities, discounted wellness services, and purchased flowers, dark chocolate, car washes, movie/theater tickets, candles, books, manicures/pedicures, and an assortment of gift certificates to recognize staff member efforts.

One staff member emailed me on July 4th to share her appreciation of the BBQ festivities we organized during lunch on July 3, 2014:

> *Hola Cathy,*
>
> *Solo queria dar las gracias por que ayer tuvimos un dia maravilloso todos. Nosotros apreciamos mucho mucho todo lo que haces por nosotros. No creo que haya otro lugar en el mundo donde sea asi como CTR. Espero que estes pasando un buen fin de semana, yo estoy haciendo tarea, pero espero acabar pronto. Muchas gracias! Eres una mujer muy fabulosa y agradezco todo tu apoyo siempre en todo. July 4, 2014.*
>
>

Claudia Ortega

> *Hi Cathy,*
>
> *I just wanted to thank you for yesterday. We all had a marvelous day. We appreciate very much all that you do for us. I do not believe that there is another place in the whole world like CTR. I hope that you have a good weekend. I am doing homework, but hope to finish soon. Many thanks! You are a fabulous woman and I appreciate always your support.*

PRINCIPLE 3: CREATE STAFF MISSION AND INCLUSIVENESS PHILOSOPHY STATEMENTS

A nonprofit mission statement is a description of an agency's reason for existence. It may provide answers to what you do, but not explicitly how you provide a service. Why am I suggesting that it is necessary to consider creating an additional statement for the staff and adopting an inclusiveness philosophy? These additional declarations will steer the daily operations of the organization and become the public demonstration of the organization's integrity and indeed "way of life." They may expedite solutions to dilemmas and assist in decision-making. Too often assumptions are made about the intentions, values, and internal functioning of the nonprofit environment.

Our employment candidates frequently, and erroneously, describe the nonprofit environment as "a very welcoming, very friendly, big disorganized family of team players who share a sacrificial spirit. Everyone is overworked and underpaid and no one really cares." Is this your staff culture? For too many of us, we haven't decided who we are or who we want to be. A staff mission statement will address your limbo.

All agency members should participate in crafting the statement—it is not a leadership exercise. Because leadership can unwittingly influence the outcome, a skilled facilitator may be helpful in developing both statements. The enterprise requires a thoughtful and broad-spectrum approach. Consider how you define and share your commitments to clients/customers, how you define and promote leadership, problem-solve, and make decisions. What is the desired culture of your agency? What kind of agency do you want to be? What do you value and want to uphold . . . in spite of everything?

Our staff mission statement states:

> *To create and maintain a cooperative work environment that promotes trust, accountability and respect for individual strengths and team growth, while maintaining a commitment to a common vision (1994).*

Our inclusiveness philosophy states:

> *The Center for Trauma & Resilience is an inclusive agency which values the contributions and cultures of all its stakeholders and clients. We create an organizational culture based on respect, accountability and trust. Our commitment to inclusiveness is evidenced by our agency's policies, practices and strategic plans (2008).*

We have learned that a regular review of both statements is beneficial, especially if we find ourselves embroiled in a conflict or impasse. Every new hire is asked to respond to our staff mission statement and our inclusiveness philosophy. We want to be clear, and every employee is entrusted with upholding and mirroring the values set forth in both statements.

PRINCIPLE 4: ATTEND TO AGENCY INCLUSIVENESS AND RECOGNITION OF HISTORICAL TRAUMA

CTR staff members (and board members) mirror the gender, age, ethnicity, sexual orientation, and linguistic and religious diversity of the metropolitan Denver community. It is an intensely intentional environmental design that has been recognized and celebrated. A number of employees throughout the years have distinguished our diverse and inclusive environment as an unrecognized benefit of self-care.

Real-Life EXAMPLE

Daiga, a six-year employee who is Latvian, said, "This is the first time in my 20-year employment history that anyone encouraged me to celebrate Latvia Day! My former employers weren't interested in my small country . . . they felt more comfortable believing I was Russian or something like that!"

In 1987, during the agency's inception, racial/ethnic diversity was solicited. The convening board and management desire to reflect multiculturalism was part of the dream. The "colored" faces at the organization remained steady. There was always *at least one person* who could be asked to represent a *minority* community. The organization administrators were so proud of themselves, not realizing their practice trivialized and tokenized staff members. The idea of integrating whole people, not just their "faces," was unrecognized and typically discussed as an additive approach. For example:

- **Education:** "We must include one session on how to serve diverse communities."

- **Event planning:** "We should ask a Native American to provide the opening prayer and libation ceremony."

- **Entertainment:** "Let's close our event with African drumming or a mariachi band!"

- **Membership:** "Who can we ask? Who has a high enough profile in the African-American, Latino, or LGBT community? Does anyone know her/him?"

They were so proud of themselves . . . at least they considered *"others."*

Follow a Path of Inclusiveness

In 2001, The Denver Foundation led the conversation to address the role of race and ethnicity and its impact on nonprofit effectiveness with community engagement. The foundation addressed the paucity of people of color on nonprofit staffs, boards, and serving as donors and volunteers. The Foundation findings reported that "in case studies of highly inclusive organizations, either a founding CEO or new CEO with a strong commitment to inclusiveness had dramatically influenced the organization's culture." (The Denver Foundation, 2003).

The Foundation illuminated research and provided guidance, consultants, conferences, and funding to nonprofits interested in growing their inclusiveness efforts. In 2006, CTR was awarded (along with 11 others) a two-year grant to create an inclusiveness blueprint. Our ultimate goal was to develop and *institutionalize inclusive policies, protocols, and practices* throughout the agency, in order for inclusiveness to live beyond the current agency administration.

Acknowledge Historical Trauma in Our Clients and Employees

As an African American and clinician steeped in trauma and crime victim services, I acknowledge the manifestation of historical trauma and its significance for both our clients and employees. Maria Yellow Horse Brave Heart defines historical trauma as the "cumulative emotional and psychological wounding over the life span and across generations, emanating from massive group trauma." (Brave Heart and DeBruyn, 1998). Although her work primarily focused on Native Americans, specifically Lakota peoples, she says that intergenerational trauma definitions meet the 1948 United Nations General Assembly definition of genocide. (Brave Heart and DeBruyn, 1998). Brave Heart points to a constellation of features: sadness, depression, trauma fixation, preoccupation with ancestral suffering or loyalty, and living in both the past and present as common psychological conditions for the Lakota, along with Jewish people as a result of the Holocaust and African Americans suffering the aftermath of slavery. She reports that a history of chronic losses is collaborated with psychic numbing, elevated mortality, and difficulty moving forward.

In *Post Traumatic Slave Syndrome*, Dr. Joy DeGruy Leary agrees and postulates that the historical trauma of slavery and post-slavery conditions (such as black codes, convict leasing, and Jim Crow laws) can be traced to current "survival" behaviors of African Americans that negatively impact our mental and physical health, disrupt family and relationship patterns, and result in self-sabotage and self-destructive activities. (Leary, 2005).

The work of Brave Heart and DeGruy Leary has added another dimension to the discipline of trauma recovery, vicarious trauma, and trauma-informed practices.

In late 1997, Denver was selected as a site for a coveted multiyear grant to launch victim services in the new millennium—Victim Services 2000! In 2001, the Denver Victim Services Network, a collaboration of 30 victim assistance agencies, adopted a statement about vicarious traumatization. The statement initially read:

> *Vicarious trauma is a term used to describe the thoughts, feelings, and behaviors that can result from the repeated exposure to the trauma of others. As people who work with victims of crime, we acknowledge the impact our work has on us, personally and professionally, on our organizations and on the victims we serve. The compassion we draw upon to do our work increases our risk to experience vicarious trauma.* (Denver District Attorney Victim Services Network, 2001).

Upon review, a handful of people of color (the very few who were victim advocates) contested the statement that was written by primarily Caucasian victim service providers. They protested and advocated that the philosophy statement be expanded to recognize the effects of racism, as well as the legacy of hate and disenfranchisement endured by people of color. The statement was amended to read:

> *In addition, it is imperative to recognize cultural differences, and the*
> *experiences of historically oppressed groups may further compound*
> *the trauma of both the victim and the service provider. Therefore, it is*
> *incumbent on us to recognize our vulnerability and take steps to prevent*
> *and address vicarious trauma at both the individual and agency levels. We*
> *believe that self-care is a skill that can be learned and we are committed to*
> *practicing self-care in order to nurture and sustain healthy organizations.*
> (Denver District Attorney Victim Services Network, 2001).

I urge agencies to commit to inclusiveness by embracing all perspectives and contributions, not just token representation. The best practice approach as outlined by The Denver Foundation is not a quick fix, colorblind, or "festivity" driven. (The Denver Foundation, 2003). Beware of short-term activities where the identified purpose is designed to introduce staff members to learn about historical figures such as Cesar Chavez (whose birthday is a recognized holiday by our agency and the city of Denver), the clichéd potluck of "soul food" during African-American history month, or the "tell us all about *your culture* events."

In 1989, legal scholar Kimberlé Crenshaw proposed the term *intersectionality* (of racism, sexism, homophobia, transphobia, ableism, xenophobia, classism, etc.) and explored their interconnectedness and proposed that they cannot be examined separately from one another. Our work must address the whole person. (Crenshaw, 1989; Crenshaw, 1991).

Since 2004, our effort to build an inclusive organization has resulted in the creation of:

- A critical mass of racially/ethnically, linguistically, religiously, etc., diverse staff, volunteers, interns, and board members.
- An inclusiveness philosophy that stands alongside our agency mission and self-care statement.
- New-hire "inclusiveness" orientation that addresses anti racism and a variety of oppressions, micro-aggressions, and injustices.

- Annual training for staff and board members on inclusiveness, and anti racism and a variety of oppressions, micro-aggressions, and injustices.

- Annual ethical communication training to share values and codes of conduct while working interpersonally or electronically.

- A book/film club—materials are chosen to raise consciousness (participation is voluntary).

- A standing inclusiveness committee dedicated to planning quarterly educational conversations/experiences aimed at broadening our historical, social, and cultural knowledge.

- Annual recognition of cultural events, such as Día de los Muertos.

- A small on-site library of books and films. (All staff members are encouraged to provide recommendations for further discussion and study.)

I have learned that an inclusive, actualized staff will call into action controversial or high-profile issues on matters of social injustice.

Real-Life EXAMPLE

In May 2006, there was a call for a "national boycott" by immigrants. One staff member, Lucia, broached this protest during our supervision and shared her ambivalence with me. She identified as Latina and wished to participate in the boycott, but did not want to be deceptive and call in "sick." She stated she was proud of our agency and our commitment to inclusiveness, yet she felt called to express her solidarity and march with her ethnic community. I suggested, and she agreed, that we bring the issue to the full staff for discussion. The discussion was enlightening. There were Latinos who had no intention of participating; white staff members who expressed confusion about the issue; and one African-American staff member who wondered, "If there was a similar call for boycott for African Americans, would the agency support it?" During the meeting, staff questioned what would happen to the crime victims we served—the majority being immigrants/people of color—if the agency "closed"?

The final outcome was that any prospective participant was welcome to have the day off to participate in the demonstration. Staff members who planned to work, but wished to be supportive, were given recommendations (for example, wear white clothing and agree not to purchase anything on that day) to demonstrate their support.

Real-Life EXAMPLE

In March 2015, a local therapist requesting to be added to our agency therapist resource directory reacted negatively to our stated preferences for new applicants.

We stated: *The Center has limited capacity to integrate new therapists who want to be part of the therapy referral system. Currently, we have approximately 150 therapists in the database. At this time, we are seeking therapists who meet one or more of the following criteria:*

- *Has specific and demonstrated ethnic or cultural experience*
- *Speaks Spanish*
- *Offers free consultations and a sliding scale to $40*
- *Accepts Victim Compensation as full payment, accepts Medicaid or other insurance*
- *Is a male therapist*
- *Offers home visits*

The therapist responded: "So, since I am a white, English-speaking female who for safety and client confidentiality reasons prefers to see clients in my office and cannot afford to do a session for $40, I will not even be considered, even though I have almost 40 years of experience?"

We replied: *"We are expanding our resource directory to better meet the needs of client requests. We currently have over 150 people who have your similar qualifications. At this time we are addressing priority areas to better align with the needs of the people we serve."*

Additionally, we provide our "How to Choose a Therapist Checklist" and encourage clients (staff or volunteers) to approach this powerful (and expensive) intervention thoughtfully. The checklist asks prospective therapy candidates to consider *their preferences* in terms of "race/ethnicity, age, sexual orientation, language, location, accessibility, etc. when choosing a therapist."

Quarterly, we invite interested therapists to meet and greet the program staff and share their therapeutic orientation and areas of expertise, and yes, we ask them about how they care for themselves—self-care!

Emotional Intensity, Passion, Fierceness, and—Ultimately—Insight and Healing

Leadership should anticipate that agency inclusiveness events will produce tears, fears, confusion, anger, lots of discussion, and, hopefully, insight. It is a complex and intricate journey that begins with relearning history, as Howard Zinn stated in his book *A People's History of the United States*, from the people's perspective. It inspires hope and healing. It is a learning process wherein staff members engage, bringing their collective biological, emotional, psychological, generational, and cultural histories to enhance understanding and to broaden our professional selves. (Zinn, 1980).

These collective histories and experiences produce emotional intensity, passion, and fierceness that may cause some agency staff members to feel vulnerable or intimidated. In their article "Cultural Ways of Learning: Individual Traits or Repertoires of Practice," Gutiérrez and Rogoff assert that an individual's and group's experience with certain activities, not necessarily their ethnic group membership, may impact their engagement and experience. (Gutiérrez & Rogoff, 2003). Careful, respectful, and *factual* dialog must be the foundation in order to navigate these discussions. Otherwise, animosity and conflict, hurt feelings, and staff triangles will certainly be the outcome.

During supervision, a relatively new hire, a 23-year-old Caucasian woman, a former intern, inquired, "Is there a role for white people in this agency?" When I probed further, she stated she felt "like everyone was a person of color." It was an unusual situation for her, and she felt uneasy. Of the 13 staff members, six were white, and of those six, one was Muslim, one was

Latvian, one was bilingual (Spanish speaking). She immediately realized she had not considered them, because they were not "regular white people." We had a lengthy conversation on her anxiety and question.

She later reflected on our supervision:

> As I entered into supervision, I had many thoughts and feelings stirring about my place at the agency. I had grown up in an environment where I was the majority and, honestly, the only race. I had been told that my abilities were limitless, and there were continuous messages about how I could do anything I put my mind to. My employment at CTR started to challenge these ideas. I thought I could and would help anyone; little did I know not everyone wanted my help.
>
> It was difficult at first to understand why I was not the best fit for counseling or group work with individuals who were primarily people of color. I had never been told that I couldn't do or get whatever I wanted. I went into supervision wondering what my role was if I couldn't speak Spanish or if I was viewed as a person who "has no culture."
>
> It became apparent to me quickly that I was the minority at the agency, and that was scary only because it was a new experience. It would have been easy to become offended by this, and it can still sometimes be a challenge to not go there. However, I saw the impact and change that an African-American counselor could have with a group of African-American students compared to me, a white counselor. I also saw our ability as an agency to build instant rapport by accommodating the desire of the client for race and gender of a therapist.
>
> If I was honest with myself, I knew why I was the minority, because it is the reality of the need. I came to my supervisor with this question of is there a role for me, as a white person, in an agency with so much diversity.
>
> It continues to be something I process, but I see that I do have value and I also see the importance of why the agency looks like it does. Her response was helpful as she explained that if she wanted the agency to be all people of color, it would be so and that she was intentional in choosing me for my position. It made me realize that I do have a place, and that a lot of my insecurities stemmed from my entitlement being crushed. I understand this entitlement had good intentions of wanting to help people and oftentimes it goes unrecognized because it hides behind good intentions. However, the

reality is, there is arrogance behind assuming that you can help anyone and that your race should not be a barrier in giving and receiving services. This was a helpful realization for me and has forced me to process this part of myself and has made me realize I do have strengths, but not in everything and not in every situation will I be the best.

Ashley Brown—employee for four years

I referred her to another Caucasian employee, who had similar insights 10 years earlier and had written a blog about her experience.

The End of Kumbaya

I began working for a small nonprofit at the age of 24. The staff was more diverse than anyplace I had ever been; the clients were much more diverse than anyplace that I had ever worked. All of a sudden race and ethnicity were in the forefront of my everyday life. It was stressful and I didn't know why. Remember, I came from the 1980s where I was part of a rainbow coalition. Even though we looked different on the outside, deep down we were all the same. If we would all just believe this, we were going to be fine! History be damned, we were all people helpers with the goal of making this world a better place and things were on the way up. These were the days of "diversity training" where we learned that the bad names that some people called each other were "just the tip of the iceberg." I went to the trainings and was bombarded with stories of hatred and cruelty both in the past and in the present day. I felt white guilt, lots of it. Then I felt guilty but somewhat justified with my thoughts of how people of color had it bad but their start was not that much different than white immigrant communities. I struggled, denied, and struggled some more.

*Why were the people of color talking about needing supportive services for their communities? I would help anyone; I didn't care what color they were. My privilege was truly blinding. **My supervisor suggested that maybe I didn't care what color my clients were, but my clients cared what color I was.** It rocked my world. I am nice, caring, smart, respectful, helpful and hardworking. I am true to my word and give my best to anyone I work with. Why would it matter to them if I was white? If my heart was in the right place, why did color matter? Race seemed to work its way into everything. I could feel my whiteness and I also realized that so could those around me. It felt that discussions about anything—services,*

programs, organizations, fundraising, volunteers, board members—always
came around to race. I struggled, I resisted, and then I started reading. I
read stories about people's histories written by the people who had lived
them. I learned about what it was like and what others had endured to get
to where they were. I opened myself up, no longer questioning "why" but
understanding it as a given. I was blessed and privileged to be taken into
the company of women who trusted and shared with me their stories and
perceptions. I realized that what I had been experiencing was transference/
countertransference. Carl Jung states that within the transference dyad both
participants typically experience a variety of opposites; that in love and in
psychological growth, the key to success is the ability to endure the tension
of the opposites without abandoning the process, and that this tension
allows one to grow and to transform. I went back to what I know. I believe
that the essence of a good relationship is built on mutual respect and trust.
In order to build mutual respect and trust, I needed to acknowledge and
honor our differences.

Kathi Fanning, employee for 22 years

I encourage leadership/management to set aside time for staff to process
these musings. One of the tools we employ is providing time to "debrief" a
week following any scheduled inclusiveness event and contracting with an
exceptionally skilled facilitator (if necessary) to guide the conversation to
address any reactivity.

PRINCIPLE 5: OFFER CLINICAL AND PROGRAM SUPERVISION

The provision of clinical supervision by an *experienced* licensed supervisor
is an asset that agency directors may skimp on or overlook in trauma
advocacy programs. However, this is a mistake, as clinical (and program)
supervision enable staff to attain new knowledge, reflect on their practice,
examine any ethical dilemmas or professional struggles, and gain support
for positive or difficult interactions and decisions.

Engage a Professional Clinician from Outside the Agency

I believe a professional who will not be compromised as an employee of
the agency best serves the clinical supervision purpose. Experts agree that
organizations that treat the traumatized should provide opportunities

for *regular* supervision, consultation, and case discussion. (Pearlman & Saakvitne, 1995b; Figley, 1995). Regardless of whether agency counseling staff members have advanced degrees, hold licenses, or are solely hotline interventionists/case managers, at some point every individual will be negatively impacted by the traumatic material that they are routinely seeing and hearing.

I have observed that for new hires (and interns), the façade of personal safety and obliviousness they enjoyed starts to falter after four months of direct service. They begin to exhibit symptoms of anxiety and negativity. They see potential crimes, danger, and threatening criminal behavior around every corner.

- "Why is the Center located so close to a high-crime area?"

- "I read that someone was robbed/assaulted/raped near here last month!"

- "Is it safe to park my scooter in this neighborhood?"

They transfer their anxiety to clients and begin to question the validity of the client's victimization.

- "I am not really sure if his rent money was stolen. The landlord says he has trouble collecting his rent and that he is late every month!"

- "Why should we change her locks? She will only give her boyfriend the key."

- "I don't think they really want help. They never return my calls."

- " I think violence is more acceptable in their culture."

- "Why did she go grocery shopping at night?"

Clinical Supervision Is Not a Substitute for Personal/Individual Therapy

Clinical supervision and collegial talks help workers steady their perspective and normalize their new lens on the world. However, clinical supervision is *not* a substitute for personal/individual therapy. It is tempting for staff to try to circumvent doing their own work. The wise counsel of a clinical consultant comes in handy here.

I have found that the two processes enhance each other. Personal therapy advances the notion of "buying what you sell," and clinical supervision helps staff members to identify where their personal and professional endeavors merge. The clinical supervisor provides guidance and signposts for those staff members whose performance may be negatively impacted by agency work or by other personal/relational issues. Clinical supervisors support staff to traverse these minefields and subsequently head off program implosion.

Deal with Dual or Emotionally Intense Relationships with Clients

People of color and other communities of historically oppressed groups may quickly find themselves in dual or emotionally intense relationships with clients. They may share histories of mistrust, betrayal, violence, or medical, occupational, and social abuses, and become acutely aware of resemblances in their own lives.

Regardless of ethnicity, staff members who share similar life circumstances with their clients will be impacted. The impact may manifest in a range of behaviors, such as rescuing/inability to recognize boundaries to a reluctance or refusal to provide services. For example, a staff member whose spouse lived for a period of time in a refugee camp recognized that she was unable to provide services to members from the colonizer's country.

The first step in caring for affected staff members is recognition that a historical injury has taken place. The second step is affirmation and support. The third step may involve facilitating access to interventions that buffer the effects of trauma and support healing. (Tully, 1999, p. 31). The staff member's cultural beliefs and history will play a role in the health-seeking behavior. (This will also be true for clients.) It is essential to provide traditional resources as well as indigenous complementary therapies. The chosen interventions might include culture-specific practices such as indigenous/traditional purification ceremonies, herbs, baths, drumming, song, dance, art, ritual prayers, cleansings, and/or storytelling.

Hold Mandatory Case Management Meetings

Why mandatory meetings? Couldn't staff find a better use for two hours of meetings? Perhaps they prefer to serve additional clients or catch up on paperwork. Case management meetings are important because isolation and lack of or limited collegial support are believed to contribute to vicarious traumatization. (McCann and Pearlman, 1990).

Judith Herman says it best: "The core experiences of psychological trauma are disempowerment and disconnection from others. Recovery, therefore, is based upon the empowerment of the survivor and the creation of new connections. Recovery can take place only within the context of relationships; it cannot occur in isolation." (Herman, 1992, p. 133).

It is our hope that any healing intervention addresses disempowerment and disconnection and focuses on reconnecting to one's own power and the fellowship of others. Biweekly, our clinical consultant oversees the counseling team case management meetings. Case presentations are organized by categories such as *high-profile/high-risk, unusual situation, media issue; community issue; professional struggle;* and *success stories.* At these mandatory gatherings, staff members (and interns) present a client and his or her victimization experience and provide their assessment, interventions, and case management plan.

Other staff members prepare questions to advance their own knowledge or expand the knowledge of their peers. Staff share personal or professional struggles, problem-solve, highlight new community resources, and act as sounding boards for each other. All counseling personnel are required to attend and required to present cases at these meetings.

Contemporaneous with individual clinical supervision and the biweekly group case presentation is an agency protocol that permits anyone to convene a "critical incident briefing." It is a best practice that has served the agency well between regularly scheduled individual supervisions. The following are real-life examples of a critical incident request and process.

Real-Life EXAMPLE

Naima, a new staff member, was scheduled for her second hotline shift. She was asked by another counselor to follow up with a caller on a crime scene that required the scheduling of a "cleanup service" following the suicide of an elderly man. As the new counselor read the case notes, she quickly realized that she knew the deceased. He was an elderly gentleman who had patronized the coffee shop where she worked on a part-time basis. Naima was shaken and tearful after reading the case. The counselor enacted the critical incident protocol. All of the counseling staff gathered later that afternoon to provide support to this new staff member.

Real-Life E X A M P L E

A staff member, Kimberly, was out of state attending a conference when she learned from a colleague, attending the same conference, that a former client for whom she had provided legal immigration assistance had been murdered by her ex-spouse, leaving behind their young daughter. Kimberly contacted her supervisor. She was extremely upset and in tears. She and her supervisor discussed ways to cope and get support until she returned to the office.

After Kimberly returned to the office, a critical incident briefing was held. We learned that a number of staff members had been similarly impacted and included the counselor who facilitated a women's group in which the deceased had participated, as well as the children's counselor who had worked with the deceased's daughter prior to her decision to leave the abusive relationship. The front office staff had greeted the now-deceased client every week when she arrived at the agency for services. All were able to share experiences and benefit from group support.

Provide Program Supervision

Why would an organization need program supervision if clinical supervision exists? Program supervision is primarily concerned with getting goals and objectives accomplished and improving the effectiveness and efficiency of employee tasks. Program supervisors become the point of contact and resource to help supervisees interface successfully with co-workers, community relations, and agency systems, as well as anything that affects an employee's ability to successfully perform his or her job functions.

It is fundamental for all staff members to be engaged in regular, ongoing conversations about their performance, which include the topics of acclimating to the agency environment and engaging in self-care. Regular supervision allows employees an opportunity to recommend program enhancements and vent about any obstacles that interfere with achieving their program goals.

I always share my supervision philosophy with supervisees. I customize my approach to each individual. I can offer supervision that is "just give me the facts," or I can offer a style that is more growth- and leadership-oriented and involves more prodding. Generally I state my expectation that supervisees bring items to discuss because it is not the "Cathy Phelps show." I remind the individuals of the agency's expectation (written in all job descriptions) that *every* employee annually recommend at least one agency/program enhancement.

At CTR, supervisors meet with all new hires *every week* during their four-month orientation/probation period. Subsequently, I recommend twice-a-month meetings, depending on the staff member's request or the supervisor's confidence in the employee. The primary focus is to assist the employee to thrive.

Real-Life EXAMPLE

I had convinced myself that seasoned or senior staff members were content with "supervision on the fly" (for example, answering questions or responding via email, commenting on items as we passed each other in the hallway or conference room, and after reviewing their monthly reports, noting that they were on track with their self-care). I rationalized that tenured employees really did not want or need regular supervision. I was wrong. I learned that these staff members missed our supervision and their opportunity to sit, discuss, and just check in with me. They felt shortchanged. I rectified the situation, and now meet with the tenured staff members no less than once a month.

If an agency is truly a lifelong learning institution, there will always be something to discuss with employees.

PRINCIPLE 6: DESIGN CONFLICT RESOLUTION POLICIES AND ESTABLISH BOUNDARIES

Defining conflict can be tricky. Is one person's venting, another person's ruminating, and yet another's sneering about an issue the definition of unresolved conflict? Does anyone like dealing with conflict among personnel? If so, I haven't met that individual. I have learned that management's inability to identify, address, and resolve conflict quickly escalates negativity, obstructionist behaviors, and conflict triangles.

During the agency interview process, job candidates typically offer a perfect recipe response on managing conflict but then neglect to use their recipe when they find themselves at odds with another colleague or supervisor.

Create and Adopt a Conflict Resolution Policy

Our agency adopted a conflict resolution policy and protocol, and all new hires are oriented to the policy. Every employee signs the memo that states that he or she has read and understands the policy and agrees to abide by the process. It is not a universal remedy or cure-all, but it does offer guidance for managing workplace drama. A conflict policy allows management to instruct or discipline involved parties (and connivers) who ignore the protocol. Our conflict resolution policy (see Figure 10.3) instructs "third parties" to interrupt the conflict, and it has been a tool that minimizes triangling at our agency. Third parties can be held similarly accountable for participating in any conflict.

FIGURE 10.3 ■ **Conflict Resolution Policy**

THE CENTER FOR TRAUMA & RESILIENCE
CONFLICT RESOLUTION GUIDELINES

A. COMMUNICATION AT THE CENTER
   1. Directly offer constructive feedback.
   2. Share relevant information and try new ideas.
   3. Be accountable for your wants, needs, and boundaries in the workplace.
   4. Actively listen to other's opinions considering both facts and feelings.
   5. Be courteous and cooperative.
   6. Actively participate in retreats, meetings, and discussions by giving feedback when asked without fear of reprisal.
   7. Be accountable for your participation in the conflict resolution process.

B. SUGGESTIONS FOR CONFLICT RESOLUTION
   1. These guidelines do not supersede the Center's policies and procedures.
   2. When dealing with conflict resolution:
      C larify ▸ **A** cknowledge ▸ **V** erify ▸ **E** mpathize ▸ **S** ummarize
   3. Be assertive and direct. Go to the person with whom you are in conflict. Deal with conflict in a calm, open, and immediate (if possible) fashion.
   4. While meeting with the person with whom you are in conflict, share information and feelings to gain knowledge.
   5. If the issue cannot be resolved, agree to disagree or ask for help from a person willing to serve as a mediator.
   6. If you find you are a third party to a conflict:
      a. Redirect the person (first party) back to the person with whom they have the conflict (second party).
      b. When the third party is concerned that conflict issues remain unresolved, the third party should attempt to act as an informal mediator between the persons in conflict. Information must be shared within the threesome, but should not go beyond.
      c. ALL PARTIES—STOP HERE! Do not go to a fourth party. If necessary, encourage the persons in conflict to use formal mediation or grievance procedures as detailed in personnel policies.

Rev 04/06

When disagreements arise, as they inevitably will, painstaking attention needs to be paid to the resolution process. Leadership should be prepared to address conflict as quickly as possible to reduce gossip, acting-out behaviors, and the sabotage that too often accompanies it. Containment is the key.

Silence Can Be a Symptom of Conflict

Do not be fooled into believing that because things appear to be quiet, conflict doesn't exist. My favorite example is from an employee who shared with me during supervision that when there was public disagreement at any staff gathering, she pretended to "become part of the upholstery." She stated she rarely added her voice and merely tried to disappear. It was many years ago, but I still chuckle when I recall that supervision meeting. I had no idea she was so uncomfortable. I had observed her quietness, but it did not appear abnormal behavior for her.

All voices are valued, and all should weigh in on plans that affect the agency environment. Employees who may be feeling upset, irritated, or angry (about any number of things) and wish to disengage may attempt to avoid communicating. Silence or lack of a response are red flags and pose a problem for management.

Real-Life E X A M P L E

Following the separation of a charismatic, manipulative, and problematic employee, I asked the agency clinical consultant to facilitate a special staff meeting so that staff members could express their thoughts and concerns. (It is a practice I employ whenever someone is separated from the agency.) I opened the meeting by stating that, while I would be as transparent as possible, there were human resource limitations to some of the questions I could answer.

The 15 staff members sat silently for a long while. There were a few mumblings and vocalizations, but mostly it was quiet. One person stated that she didn't have anything to say. Another person said she disagreed with the discharge and stated that in the last three years, a few people that she liked had resigned or been separated.

(Continued)

I had previously overheard snippets of conversations—pro and con—about my decision. So, I decided to ask everyone at the table to state if they had any thoughts and said that I wanted to hear from everyone. I asked each staff member to be accountable for him or herself. One person stated that she "really liked the discharged employee, but agreed that he was no longer a fit with the agency values." Another staff member expressed that "he *needed* to go" and was "relieved that he is gone." And, one individual stated she was "unhappy with the meeting and disliked being compelled to speak." We processed information and feelings for an hour. I shared my investment and commitment to each employee and stated that it was ultimately my call to make decisions that were difficult and at times unpopular.

Real-Life E X A M P L E

Several staff members were annoyed following a decision to hire a person from outside the agency for a newly designed position. Two current employees had applied for the position. We had processed the hiring team's decision at a previous meeting. However, during a subsequent staff meeting, the unhappiness with my decision appeared to affect an unrelated event.

I asked staff members if they wanted to celebrate the agency's anniversary with cake and invite friends/family members. Although there were some vocalizations of affirmation, a few employees were mumbling, silent, or pretended to ignore my question. As a result, I was not sure if people wanted to celebrate, wanted a cake, wanted to invite family members, or wanted to skip the whole thing. I decided to ask everyone at the table to state if they had an opinion on the matter. It felt ridiculous to engage staff at that level. However, after everyone responded, we had clarity on who wanted what. The result was not to host a special celebration but simply to have cake at a staff meeting. Afterward I met with every individual who exhibited negativity and disrespectful behavior. I listened again to their disappointment and allegiance to current employees and once again, I affirmed the hiring team's decision.

Most of the time, conflict is not silent, or hidden; it is public and involves more than two people in an agency (which is why our policy holds the third person accountable). A few examples of conflict and disagreements with leadership where I had to have "the talk" with employees:

- When 6 of 15 staff members were expectant parents, several decided to lobby for on-site childcare at the agency. Our policies and insurance liabilities were clear; it was not permissible. However, the involved parties continued to complain and paint the agency leadership as "insensitive."

- A staff member, who lived more than 45 minutes from the agency, petitioned to change the workday from 8 to 10 hours allowing a 4-day week. She lobbied other staff members to vote for her idea— after being told it was not feasible.

- When a staff member was separated or "encouraged to resign," the remaining cohort members behaved in a rude, unkind, and unhelpful manner with the new hires.

- Two staff members ignored a supervisor's directive to cease hosting groups for an agency with fewer than the required number of children. They wrote emails to co-workers in an attempt to manipulate and embarrass the supervisor.

During all of these instances, I spoke to each staff member individually and reiterated the policy/practice decision to the full agency. I reminded members of our staff mission statement and referenced their signed conflict management agreement. I insisted that the behavior cease. And, I offered to accept their resignations if they were unable to resolve their concerns.

Managing conflict is not anyone's favorite activity, but I promise you, conflict avoidance will nullify any health-promoting infrastructure. Trying to become part of the upholstery may be one way to cope with public conflict, but it is not very effective. If conflict is avoided, it will run amok, consuming more time and energy than you ever imagined. If avoided, conflict will sprout and occur so frequently that you may begin to believe you are a professional mediator or "parent in disguise" to an agency of adults.

Provide "Ethical Communication" Training

As Benjamin Franklin said, "an ounce of prevention is worth a pound of cure." Provide ethical communication training as a complement to your established conflict resolution policy. This training supports new learning and offers communication skills that staff members may not yet possess. Annually this communication training serves as a good refresher for all staff members who prefer conflict avoidance, lashing out, or believe that they can resolve disputes via email. I suggest carefully interviewing local consultants and giving them a full profile of the staff along with the agency philosophy and culture.

Separate Staff from Agency When Necessary

Conflict can easily go underground. If a disgruntled staff member has been extended opportunities to resolve differences and yet remains steadfast in his or her discontent, it is time for the individual to move on, away from the agency. Have I held these conversations? Yes. Are they difficult? Always. Inevitable? This question remains to be seen by both leadership and affected employees.

As a caveat: It is vital to distinguish for all staff members the difference between the agency conflict-resolution process and the filing of a formal grievance. Formal grievances, which may allege discriminatory, illegal, or unethical activity by a staff member or management, may require a separate protocol and/or board directive.

PRINCIPLE 7: ENSURE THE AGENCY PROVIDES A SAFE ENVIRONMENT—PHYSICALLY AND PSYCHOLOGICALLY

First and foremost, focus on safety. The agency environment should emanate physical and psychological safety for employees and clients.

Ensure Physical Safety

During the new-hire orientation and then annually, leadership should review all safety procedures with staff.

Crisis work is unpredictable and can be volatile, and attention should be given to policies that minimize risk to staff or clients. A safety binder that merely sits on a shelf will not support staff in time-sensitive or chaotic moments. Dynamic safety procedures are critical to a worker's sense of well-being. Safety planning should endeavor to prepare for a variety of situations, both inside and outside of the office, that may involve threats to staff, in person, by telephone, or by other electronic media.

I strongly urge management to review safety protocols with staff. This investment contributes to workers feeling considered and cared for in an environment that may become unstable. We have implemented the following safety and security protocols and I suggest the same for your agency:

- *Purchase a panic button.* All personnel should be instructed on what to do if the button is activated. There are no exceptions (crying wolf). If the button is activated and the procedure is to call 911, then 911 should be called. During tests or demonstrations of the panic button, be sure to notify everyone that the test will occur.

- *Offer classes on cardiopulmonary resuscitation (CPR), basic first aid, and universal precautions.* This is a wise investment for any agency that serves the public and provides practical skills for everyone working in the community.

- *Schedule an annual fire inspection. Practice fire drills and other evacuations of your team, program participants, or floor.* Implement all recommendations from the fire department. Fire drills are a critical task for residential programs or shelters.

- *Role-play agency safety protocols.* What happens if a weapon is brandished, someone begins screaming, or someone receives a threatening telephone call, letter, or email? Unfortunately, we have experienced all of these scenarios and now address them in our safety trainings.

- *Design communication protocols for personnel who provide home visits, off-site services, or on-call coverage.* Staff members must prescreen all clients, complete the lethality checklist, and be accompanied by a second staff member or intern when providing in-home services. On-call direct service staff have a management team member on call with them for administrative backup. Staff members have access to all pertinent telephone numbers.

- *If your agency's location is confidential, ensure all staff, volunteers, visitors, and clients are informed.* Staying abreast of Internet maps and search tools is recommended.

- *Attend to any security breach (for example, broken windows, lost keys, or security codes) and require a planned response prior to their occurrence.* Staff members sign a compliance agreement with agency safety protocols. Without exception, a lost key requires the rekeying of entrances and exits; any repairs are made immediately.

- *Purchase and regularly update safety or surveillance equipment and educate all staff on its usage.* Biannually, conduct a test of smoke alarms, cameras, panic buttons, and safety procedures.

Address the issue of intimate partner violence

The crime of intimate partner violence (domestic violence) may occur with anyone, anywhere, and leadership should be prepared for the moment when a staff member or volunteer is involved in or witnesses a violent or abusive relationship. Intimate partner violence is pervasive and democratic. It is important that this realization be acknowledged at the outset. Acknowledgment will reduce any associated shame or secrecy and ultimately help to protect the primary victim(s) and the entire staff.

Our process (which a few of my colleagues consider controversial) is as follows: Once anyone, staff member or volunteer, is aware that there is an abusive relationship, the informed person will be counseled to report the incident to a supervisor or the executive director. (Some proponents believe that the "crime" is a personal one and to notify leadership is an unwelcome intrusion.) Support and advocacy are offered to primary parties. However, all those affected are encouraged to avail themselves of personal/professional counseling and local resources, including protective orders.

During the last 12 years, we had two separate incidents of staff members who were stalked by abusive partners. We posted the individual's photo and vehicle description inside the agency. A safety plan was customized for each incident. Typically, however, the entire staff shall be informed of the need to be vigilant.

If further safety planning is required, we advocate a client-/staff-centered approach. *The safety of everyone on staff is at risk* should an offender attempt to threaten, stalk, become violent, or appear on agency premises. Intimate partner violence, among employees or volunteers, along with any harassing or threatening behavior, is not considered a secret or held confidential between affected parties. We know that bystanders can suffer unintended consequences of violence.

All staff members play a role in creating a safe environment

I am adamant that no employee should ever feel alone and without backup. Everyone, especially the front office receptionist, plays a role in the safety of the work environment and must be informed and protected.

Establish a "critical incident" review protocol

Agencies should have a critical incident review protocol with the primary goal of providing support to staff on any sensitive incident that negatively affects staff (or volunteers). CTR defines *critical incident* as follows:

> *A critical incident will be understood to be an incident of suicide, homicide, or other violent assault that involves a client being supported by the organization. It may also include any incident of staff or volunteer injury including sexual/domestic violence, child abuse, or other assault deemed critical to any aspect of the team.*

The timing of the review will be initiated and negotiated by interested and/or involved parties. Ideally, the review will occur as soon as possible after the traumatic (real or perceived) event happens. Any staff member can enact the protocol.

Ensure Psychological Safety

Is the work environment psychologically safe? Is it attractive and in good repair? Environmental experts agree that clean, well-lighted, organized, and aesthetically pleasing environments uplift the spirit. Conscientious leaders who spend a few dollars to frame prints (instead of posting them on the wall with pushpins); purchase live plants, art, and cultural representations of the community; and select furnishings that are colorful, comfortable, and practical will create a warm, inviting atmosphere and ambiance of wellness.

Recently, I visited 20-year-old nonprofit and was shocked to see agency signage in crayon and on cardboard. And no, it wasn't a childcare center. I am not sure how or why, but too many nonprofit environments scream, "It's good enough for the population we serve."

Do any of these items look familiar?

- Unused, broken, outdated equipment
- Torn/worn/dirty/tattered furnishings and toys
- Lost-and-found items scattered in various areas
- Stacks of dusty books/outdated magazines/journals or newsprint
- Dirty dishes, leftover food on tables
- Antiquated/broken computers/electronics
- Piles of clothes
- Grimy windows/mirrors/curtains/rugs
- Dying plants or dusty artificial ones
- Desks and file cabinets spilling over with "someday" projects
- Outdated notices on bulletin boards
- Old posters/banners/fundraising paraphernalia
- Boxes and boxes of financials or other program paperwork that has outgrown storage and now block walkways and hallways

If so, get help with cleaning, discarding, recycling, shredding, or storing. Schedule a mandatory cleaning day or find charity service volunteers looking for a one-day project. If it is broken, fix it. If it is unable to be repaired, recycle or trash it, but do *not* allow it to take up valuable workspace or be an eyesore.

A disorganized, dirty, and cluttered space (including outside porches and yards) speaks volumes. It says, "We are overwhelmed!" I imagine it could also say, "We are busy helping the people and don't have (or make) time to clean up after ourselves." Either way, support centers should refrain from broadcasting such a fact to the public. A recent visitor/client who came to our offices kept exclaiming to anyone within earshot,

> *"My goodness, I can't get over how clean, organized, and lovely this*
> *building is! In the past, when I sought services, the building was dismal.*
> *I thought to myself, Oh My God, have I come to this . . . both literally*
> *and psychologically?"*

Establish a plan to keep your environment clean

Our nonprofit has been fortunate to lease (and now own) a lovely historic Victorian-era building. We have a rotating calendar of monthly cleaning tasks (for example, yoga mats are cleaned by participants, but blankets are laundered by staff after every group series). We have on-site recycling containers and hire a monthly cleaning service for toilets, floors, and so on.

Every spring, we dedicate two eight-hour days to a *deep* cleaning of floors/ carpets, upholstery, windows, desks, counseling rooms, closets, appliances, bookshelves, and cabinets. We repot plants and clear the grounds. All agency and staff workspaces are examined. We archive and clean up personal computers, financials, files, and servers from top to bottom. Appointments are suspended (crisis services continue with the help of volunteers and interns) and, for two days, employees wear jeans or other clothes appropriate for cleaning. We divide and assign the chore list, and as a thank-you, the agency provides snacks and a tasty lunch. I confess, as a minimalist, I look forward to cleaning days! It's a chance to rethink all the clutter I have accumulated. Everyone participates and the two days become a mini–team-building exercise. Staff take pride in maintaining an organized and welcoming environment.

Establish boundaries around technology

Our work with crime victims/survivors mandates the entire agency be present and engaged with clients and colleagues. It is more than a courtesy; it is integral to respectful service.

One of the customer service boundaries we established upon the arrival of cell phones was the prohibition of talking on cell phones inside of our building—by clients, customers, volunteers, and staff. We dared to challenge the notions that everyone must be accessible at a moment's notice and that it is acceptable for anyone, at any time, to disrupt any environment.

Our agency has 18 business landlines, and we realized that incessant and uncontrolled cell phone usage was quickly deteriorating our office environment. Leadership reviewed the costs and rewards, including the temptation to "just take this call" or being distracted by new text or email photos, and learned that staff behavior was perceived as rude by clients and interfered with safety protocols. How would you feel if you were in a counseling session and your counselor's cell phone began ringing or buzzing and she felt compelled to answer, or if you noticed that your supervisor was distracted because he or she appeared to be wondering who was on the phone?

There are times when we need to take our calls from loved ones who are ill or when there is a family emergency. The societal norm, however, has become that we are permitted to make or answer cell phones anywhere and everywhere. When I polled staff about the content of the "urgent calls" that they had felt compelled to excuse themselves from a meeting to answer, some of the reasons they offered were:

- "I was checking to see if my girlfriend had lunch money."
- "I wanted to see how my child's potty training is progressing."
- "My daughter wanted to ask me if she could have pizza for lunch."
- "My son wanted to ask if he could have a sleepover."
- "My husband/wife couldn't find his/her (socks, medicine, earrings, soccer ball, fishing pole)."

Needless to say, these are not calls that needed to interrupt the workday. Endless calls and texts for these reasons make a work environment untenable.

Our office policy has been met with pouting and accusations that leadership was "old school" and "out of touch." Some of the staff members who shared offices confided in leadership that they agreed with leadership's concern. They were tired of listening to frivolous conversations and annoyed that while they were working their officemate was chatting and texting. It was not long before mutual cell phones and music selections began blaring or they used earphones (only one earphone, because both could interfere with our safety protocols) in an attempt to drown out other sounds.

Certainly, texting has contributed to a quieter environment. Our policies do not prohibit texting, but we still limit phone use during staff meetings and other professional meetings.

Members of leadership and others in private offices know how easy it is to be distracted. We understand how tempting it is to be alone in an office, chatting away on the phone, making dinner reservations, watching YouTube, or selling items on eBay. One of my colleagues told me that after he fired his immigration advocate, he discovered that in less than four months of employment, she had logged more than 300 hours on commercial shopping sites. She was online shopping for more than half of her workday, every day. Everyone assumed she was intensely working because her door was constantly closed and she rarely answered her telephone.

Establish "workday" parameters

Speaking of work, establish the workday. Staff members (and executives) are strongly discouraged from being contacted at home if they are ill, on vacation or holiday, or just because someone in the office believes they cannot function without an immediate answer to a question. Discourage the culture that intimates "we can have access to you at all times," or one that says organization (disorganization) interest trumps your personal time. Construct opportunities to cross-train staff, plan for vacations, and let staff members know that you trust them to use their problem-solving skills. Are there exceptions to this rule? Of course, and that's what they should remain—exceptions.

The workday has a beginning and end. Staff members who are connected to work email ("it just pops up on my phone") are discouraged to respond to emails around the clock. Yes, I am told that *they may still review* them—but they restrain themselves from responding.

In my 12 years as executive director, I am pleased to say that I have only been contacted about a dozen times when I was not on the proverbial clock.

PRINCIPLE 8: FORMALIZE STAFF INVOLVEMENT (A.K.A. TEAM BUILDING)

Seek staff input beyond the planning of the obligatory holiday potluck. Too often, the only time agency personnel are invited to participate in

TABLE 10.1 ■ **Ways CTR Engages Staff**

- Staff meetings
- Staff committees
- Quarterly retreats
- Expanding Nonprofit Inclusiveness events
- Potlucks for new hires, new interns, holidays, and staff/agency accomplishments
- Bring-your-child-to-work day
- Fundraisers and special events
- Board of Directors' orientation, board meetings, board committees
- Participation in interviews with prospective employees and interns
- Participation in "meet and greet" interviews with prospective therapists
- Participation with funder/foundation site visits
- Bettering the Lives of Employees and Programs (BLEAP)
- Leadership retreats

nonprofit operations is when something goes awry, and then a team-building meeting or retreat looms on the horizon.

Staff involvement is integral to the health and well-being of an agency and can be easily woven into the nonprofit's operations. Solicit employee input on a variety of levels and intervals throughout the year. Take advantage of staff ideas, energy, and budding leadership skills. Listed in Table 10.1 are some of the ways we engage staff on an annual basis.

Staff Meetings

Our agency is primarily composed of counselors and advocates for social change, so consistent mechanisms for communication are emphasized. We have a weekly all-staff meeting that lasts from 20 minutes (if there are no updates) to one hour. We gather around our conference table, and everyone is asked to check in. Typically there is no preset agenda, but personal calendars are on hand to facilitate the scheduling of events. It is a time to share agency news, professional updates, and (if desired) personal notes. We brainstorm, plan, problem-solve, and deal with minutiae. Often following the first round of sharing, someone remembers something that he or she wants to discuss. It has become a tradition to have staff "seconds" and "thirds" to satisfy these flashes. Staff meetings provide a formal time for staff to console or celebrate each other on a regularly scheduled basis.

The hour is flexible. At times we host other individuals, such as friends, students, acquaintances, or guests, who have a project, a product, or an announcement about an upcoming event. For example, a former board member personally invited all staff to a concert featuring the Grammy-award-winner and Denver resident Dianne Reeves; a new vegan caterer asked us to taste-test her products; a personal trainer introduced staff to her summer "boot camp in the park." Recently, we began viewings of *TED Talk* videos or full-length documentaries on topics related to health/food and our environment such as *Fed Up, A Guerilla Gardener in South Central LA, Food, Inc.,* and *An Inconvenient Truth.* These meetings keep staff buzzing for hours and stimulate organizational and personal change.

The administrative team keeps an electronic notebook of minutes so absentees can stay informed. I have found that the notebook is a great way to quickly bring new hires up to speed on agency activities and culture.

Staff Committees

CTR has a variety of standing staff committees. Every year, staff members are required to select and serve on at least one committee. Currently we have the following committees:

- *Building/Safety Education Committee.* This committee organizes quarterly education in-services (for example, tornado protocols, office ergonomics, fire drills, winter driving). The committee may respond to environmental concerns, protocols, or projects.

- *Event/Fundraising Committee.* This committee brainstorms and implements events (for example, the agency's annual open house, support of board-led "pitch parties," and annual fundraisers).

- *Retreat Committee.* This committee organizes the rejuvenating quarterly staff events and recognizes individual staff milestones with cards (for example, baby showers, graduations, birthdays).

- *BLOG Committee.* This committee was conceived by staff members who wanted to express their views on any number of issues related to health promotion, leadership, and community concerns.

- *Expanding Nonprofit Inclusiveness Committee.* This committee organizes new-hire orientations and quarterly education/experiential forums on topics related to increasing cultural responsiveness and social justice.

- *Trauma-Sensitive Yoga Committee.* This committee coordinates yoga groups and presentations in the community.

On occasion, there may be a role for an ad hoc committee to oversee the pilot of a new program, purchase, or construction project. Currently, we have an ad hoc committee for a salad club, food flicks, and employees who are training for a local marathon. In these cases, staff members steer these one-time or time-limited events until they are completed or integrated into existing standing committees.

Quarterly Retreats

I confess that in my early years as a nonprofit employee, I groaned at the idea of attending a leadership-led, mandatory staff gathering where everyone pretended to have fun and enjoy each other. When I accepted the position as executive director, I eagerly changed the template and asked staff to create and implement staff retreats. My primary role as executive director (unless I am serving on the retreat committee) is to give the committee its annual budget and review liability concerns (for example, if skydiving is suggested).

The Retreat Committee is typically made up of individuals from various agency departments. At the beginning of the year, staff members brainstorm activities (sometimes there will be a theme that guides the yearlong activities) and distribute a list of activities that will be voted on by everyone on staff.

The top four activities become the quarterly retreats for the year and are immediately put on the calendar. Staff-designed retreats are noticeably more fulfilling than those previously organized by management, which typically focused on "how to build a better team" retreats. Our full-day retreats have included the following activities:

- West African, Latin, Bollywood dancing
- Meditation and yoga
- Amusement and waterpark visits
- Bowling
- Volleyball
- Cookouts
- Making sushi and origami
- Board games
- Facials/massages
- Whitewater rafting
- Miniature golf
- Nature hikes
- Bike rides
- Attending Chinese/Japanese tea ceremonies
- Viewing independently produced films/documentaries and conversing over coffee/tea afterward
- Touring local art galleries/museums
- Theater outings or community attractions
- Ice skating
- Scavenger hunts
- Henna parties
- Volunteering for a day with a local nonprofit such as, Project Angel Heart

Celebratory Potlucks

A new hire confessed to me, "When you stated staff members loved to eat and any reason to have a potluck was part of the culture, I didn't believe you!" We routinely host potlucks to welcome new staff members or interns, to recognize birthdays, holidays, staff accomplishments, certifications, and graduations, as well as to celebrate season changes ("Let's have a spring potluck!"). We created a potluck sign-up list to encourage variety and food paradigm balance. Potlucks have become such a regular occurrence that our *Potluck Sign-Up* was adopted as an agency form!

Bring-Your-Child-to-Work Day

I ask employees who are parents if they are interested in bringing their children to work on the nationally designated day. Typically, we schedule a tour of the agency and brief meetings with every staff member. The children are introduced to yoga, create an art project, and are escorted on a walk around the neighborhood. Lastly, we serve a light lunch or snack for the children. Over the years, depending on the age of the children and the tenure of the employee, the offer to spend a half day with their children may or may not be welcomed. One employee exclaimed, "Cathy, we have such a flexible agency, if there are gaps in our childcare, you permit us to bring our kids for a portion of the day. Our children already know our workplace!"

Fundraisers and Special Events

We have employed staff with a variety of fundraising and development titles, from grant writers to development ambassadors, special-event consultants, planned-giving officers, and fundraising coordinators. Regardless of which position was in vogue at the moment, I quickly learned that there is no substitute for a team approach, and staff input is necessary to ensure successful fundraising efforts.

Development personnel may have technical expertise, but agency staff and leadership know the agency history, donor personalities, board member fundraising skills, and agency culture. Participating in some aspect of agency fundraising is part of every staff member's job description. There are many options involved in securing a contribution, obtaining a sponsor or silent/live auction item, and purchasing or selling tickets or a table.

Leadership offers promotion training and materials and seeks input on desired staff incentives to heighten staff participation. The majority of the organizing is conducted by management and development staff, which ensures that the whole agency does not come to a standstill for special events.

On the day of an event, all staff—from the receptionist to the accountant—play a part in hosting. The actual event is considered work time, unless a staff member decides to be a ticketed guest. Employees who purchase tickets are treated as guests and excused from any obligations during the event.

Staff (as well as board members) are considered ambassadors and play a large role in shaping the event. Staff members may sell and take tickets, set up and take down chairs/tables, photograph, manage the auctions, assist catering or bar staff (if necessary), and interact with donors, colleagues, and other guests. Without fail, after we host an event, I receive a dozen calls and emails extolling the staff's helpfulness and professionalism.

Board of Directors' Committees

The role of staff with boards of directors varies from organization to organization. Many executives share their reluctance in encouraging agency staff members to have meaningful contact with board members. I feel differently. Newly hired employees are introduced at board meetings, and staff members provide monthly program presentations at board meetings, keeping board members acquainted with the dynamic aspects of our agency.

Staff presentations are an indispensable part of every new board member orientation. Oftentimes it is the staff presentations that spark the most passion and excitement for board members. Staff members may participate on a board-led committee. It is understood, however, that although employees provide input and assistance, they do not have a vote. Board members should be cognizant that their decisions affect the working lives of staff members. The more transparency the better!

Participation in Interviews with Prospective Employees

Interested staff members are invited to participate in the interview process for prospective new hires for the agency. Agency employees participate in both the first and second interviews, and they discuss and "vote" on the selection of new staff members. The program supervisor of the vacant or newly designed position and the executive director work to achieve consensus. No matter the outcome, everyone is heard.

Bettering the Lives of Employees and Programs (BLEAP)

Historically, annual program planning was met with sighs and resistance. Staff members disliked the *"bleeping"* brainstorming meeting, and especially disliked the time spent creating a wish list, only to learn that the upcoming year's budget would not support many of their requests. Reinventing program planning became a professional and personal challenge of leadership. We unveiled Bettering the Lives of Employees and Programs (BLEAP). The meeting was no longer an exercise in futility for the staff. It became a shared responsibility of staff and management to actualize the most popular items.

Usually organized by the director of training or administration, a BLEAP gathering occurs in September, prior to the drafting of the annual budget. Staff members are asked to put the two- to three-hour event on their calendar. Brainstorming and prioritizing takes energy, so the agency provides healthy snacks such as fresh fruit, yogurt, and granola.

If program planning is an inaugural event for your agency, introduce the importance and value of staff input in agency planning. Share your goals for the meeting. If it is a refurbishing of a former process, share the results of the past year's plan. Allow time to educate everyone on the new process and give staff members time to think about their ideas, wishes, and dreams for the agency as a whole, as well as for their particular program. Keep it light. It is a brainstorming event; all ideas are welcome.

There are two moderators at the meeting—a staff facilitator and a scribe who writes all generated ideas on large sheets of newsprint placed at the front of the room. These sheets are eventually posted around the room. We brainstorm under the following categories:

- Building/Environment
- Salary/Benefits
- Program/Services
- Fundraising/Public Relations
- Office Furniture/Supplies

Staff members create long lists under each category. It is an energetic exercise, with friendly amendments offered when interests overlap. After reviewing the lists, we remind everyone that staff members will have a limited number of votes (two) for each category.

Next, we screen the lists for items that we can likely beg, barter, or borrow. Finally, the abbreviated lists are typed and distributed. Everyone votes anonymously for their top priority (in every category). The results are revealed at a future staff meeting, and then we institute a plan to make it happen.

Although leadership does its best to honor the priorities, there have been two occasions during the past 12 years when a staff priority was vetoed. The first request involved altering the work hours from five eight-hour days to four 10-hour days. The second request involved a change from 9:00 a.m. to 5:00 p.m. to 8:00 a.m. to 4:00 p.m. Neither resolution was compatible with our clients or network of colleagues, and the requests were denied.

The BLEAP event is an internal model to ensure staff involvement. Staff members are encouraged to become involved externally (e.g., on community advisory councils and task forces, etc.) and to attend conferences and leadership institutes. As a result, I have witnessed individuals mature, blossom, and bring fresh perspectives to relationships/ networks both inside and outside of our organization.

Leadership Retreats

As a former program director, an off-site half-day retreat with agency leadership felt like a luxury. I decided to expand the leadership retreat practice. Twice yearly, daylong planning meetings have ensured that our leadership team feels heard and connected. All leadership members bring summary reports and we attend to any specific item needing assistance.

We have worked on time-consuming ventures such as creating the executive succession plan; reviewing the organization's code of ethics, fund development and/or strategic plans; planning for sabbaticals or leaves of absence; drafting new program protocols; analyzing potential collaborations; and dealing with complicated human resource issues. We have also reviewed and discussed books or papers that advance excellence in nonprofit principles. Leadership retreats allow for in-depth discussions and/or venting and flatten the leadership hierarchy.

PRINCIPLE 9: REQUIRE CONTINUING EDUCATION (A.K.A. STAFF TRAINING)

Personnel in a health-promoting environment will be motivated to advance promising practices to hone their skills. How does the expectation and requirement for continuing education for an entire workforce become realized when there are precious few dollars in your budget?

Find Ways to Get Discounted Prices on Training

Similarly to other nonprofits, we request scholarships, seek two-for-one registrations, and volunteer at workshops/conferences to get discounted fees. Staff members submit proposals for presentations, thereby lending their expertise and, if selected, ensuring their presence at no cost. There are dozens of webinars and online educational modules, many of them available at low or no cost.

Host In-House Clinical/Educational Sessions

What else can an agency do to further this goal? Designate time, at least once a month, to invite professionals, colleagues, and community-based organizations to make educational presentations to staff. We host a clinical in-service/education session twice a month. Leadership identifies "foundation training" for new hires, and staff members recommend "hot" topics and emerging issues. The in-service topics are enormous; there may barely be enough time during the year to accommodate interests. On occasion, leadership offers on-site language classes for staff interested in American Sign Language or Spanish, supporting both our philosophy of inclusiveness and lifelong learning.

Make Professional and Pertinent Literature Available to Staff

I recommend signing up for electronic or paper subscriptions to professional journals. I ask staff members to subscribe to newsletters or blogs that publish on a variety of topics, from grooming nonprofit professionals to how to organize for social justice or using art to translate and transform. A learning organization should motivate and stimulate.

Don't forget to sign up for offerings from local libraries and allied organizations that are geared toward educating the public.

Institute a Reading Hour

One of our most novel continuing-education practices is the weekly reading hour. A few years ago, I ventured into a new hire's office to see how she was doing and she told me that it was her "weekly reading hour." She stated that she dedicated one hour a week to read articles, watch educational videos, learn more about the agency history, or surf the Internet to supplement her knowledge on a particular topic. I implemented this practice on the spot. How marvelous to have an uninterrupted hour, once a week, where you actually read, instead of quickly scan, the material of your choice!

PRINCIPLE 10: REDESIGN THE ANNUAL EMPLOYEE REVIEW

The annual employee review is occasionally a source of dread and contention for both employees and supervisors. Yet, an annual review offers an avenue to review administrative, program, and self-care performance.

Typically when I share with administrators that self-care goals are part of an employee's standard performance review, and are valued and weighted equally with other performance measures, they gasp and say, "Are you serious?" To which I respond, "Absolutely," because our evaluation practice illuminates and seals the sincerity and seriousness of leadership buy-in to self-care.

Self-Care Goal Achievement Must Be an Integral Part of the Annual Review

Evaluations are based on pre-set goals and objectives—and self-care plans are no exception. Employees should not endure surprise expectations at the end of the year. If an area had not been identified (as problematic) during some point during the year, then supervisors should refrain from documenting the issue during the annual review.

Real-Life EXAMPLE

Carmen was intelligent and bilingual, but unceasingly argumentative and defensive, and often at the center of any minor agency conflict, and she was supervised on these issues throughout the year. (And I must mention that supervision notes—no matter how perfect your recall may be—is a best practice and will prove to be a supervisor's best friend.) I documented her behavior and had addressed the issue in our biweekly supervision. At her annual performance evaluation, she stated she was "offended and hurt" because we had been "getting along" the prior few months.

If I had been unable to provide examples and documentation of her challenges, I would have refrained from placing them on my review. She wrote a protesting statement. I attached it to her review and filed it.

Although CTR's qualitative and quantitative data reveal that poor performance in one area tends to be reflected in all others, I have not always found this to be the case. In fact, because self-care is a self-selected stretch goal, high performers will often receive an "outstanding" in executing their administrative and program goals, but only perform in an average manner with their self-care goals. Careful and considerate discussion during these year-end conversations is warranted if stellar-performing employees fall short of their own self-care performance.

Of course, as the management supervisor, you may have no complaints . . . because the "work got done." I caution, however, that there will be a cost if driven performers are not equally valuing self-care.

Real-Life EXAMPLE

Amber was rated as a superior performer year after year in her professional duties. Her self-care goals, however, hovered from "acceptable" to "needing improvement." She constantly stated to her supervisor that she was disappointed in herself, but other priorities took precedence. Needless to say, Amber began to make small mistakes, sometimes two or three times on the same project. She was irritable and defensive when attention was called to the errors.

Amber intentionally isolated herself from co-workers. She was counseled and upon recommendation from her supervisor, her summer work schedule was abbreviated (Fridays off) to "attend to personal and family matters." Within three months, she was back on track and giving both her administrative and self-care goals sufficient attention.

Staff Make Annual Program Enhancement Recommendations

One component of the agency evaluation mandates that each individual make a recommendation for program/agency enhancement. The expectation of this goal further substantiates management's interest in employee ideas. The resulting recommendations have ranged from simple to profound. Employees have recommended and implemented the framing of the staff mission statement (and we had copies placed in staff offices); organized and hosted a networking *desayuno* (breakfast) for Spanish-speaking service providers; and two people conducted a feasibility study aimed at establishing a satellite office in a nearby city.

Change or Adapt the Traditional Performance Review

If you are fortunate to have long-term employees, you both will become weary of "adding up the numbers" on a traditional performance review. Feel free to change it. I ask employees to summarize the highlights and disappointments of their year—in all the areas where they provide leadership. Then, I ask them to identify areas for their growth and development. I solicit ways in which I can support them. And (surprising to new hires), I always ask staff if they would like something new or different from me. When we sit down at the end of the year, the conversation is more lively and productive than checking off a list of their accomplishments.

CONCLUSION

An individualized self-care program cannot operate in a vacuum. Aligning the nonprofit infrastructure encourages congruence with the value of wellness. We began this journey in 2002 and have implemented these best practices along the way. As I discuss in the next chapter, the benefits are both individual and organizational.

CHAPTER 11

Organizational Benefits of Self-Care

A nonprofit agency with a direct service mission is wholly dependent upon its most valuable resource—its people. My experience, affirmed by agency statistical data, corroborates the fact that individual performance improves with a self-care program. Nonprofit executives often ask:

- "Does it positively affect the bottom line?"
- "How does a higher morale and broader lens affect a strategic/ fundraising plan?"

In the formation years, according to Susan Kenny Stevens' *Nonprofit Lifecycles: Stage-based Wisdom for Nonprofit Capacity*, the second stage is "The Start-up Stage: The Labor of Love," operating on passion and a low budget. (Stevens, 2001, p. 28). Although advised to stabilize administrative systems, governance, management, and fundraising capacity, nonprofit leadership begins to coast, trying to weather staff attrition and economic climates. No matter how many years the agency has been in existence, if the organization is unable to attain these benchmarks, innovation, inspiration, and inclusiveness will take a back seat to "just keeping the doors open."

INNOVATION, INSPIRATION, AND INCLUSIVENESS

So, how do you keep agency leaders—and by default their staff members— not merely coasting, but remaining engaged and enthusiastic after the formation period? Although I've separated them into the three categories, you will see that innovation, inspiration, and inclusiveness programs are all interconnected, each one supporting and enhancing the others. Use these ideas as springboards for conversation with your employees. What can you and your staff come up with to invigorate your specific organization, staff members, and community at large?

As shown in the following examples, staff members have initiated dynamic ideas over the past 10 years that have garnered new clients, partners, and donors, and doubled the agency's bottom line.

Innovation

CTR's innovations, described in the following sections, include: Mi Gente–VAWA Legal Solutions, The Translation & Interpreting Center, the Health Enabling for Listening Professionals (HELP) program, and Befriending the Body Trauma-Sensitive Yoga Program.

Innovation—Bringing the Language and Immigration Services In-House

In the fall of 2004, a 25-year-old nonprofit that provided a language interpreter bank and legal immigration services dissolved. There was a mountain of speculation and finger-pointing. After making a number of inquiries and begging Latino-serving nonprofits to save the agency, the director of the dissolved agency approached me. My proposal to assume these programs was barely out of my mouth when my leadership team members shouted, "We can reinvent these programs and make them successful!" My board of directors agreed. We began the journey to develop a business plan to recreate the language program as an earned-income venture and delved into legal immigration. We met with small-business owners, attended business planning workshops, and educated ourselves on immigration policy. These enterprises were doubly important because they aided CTR's ability to be more inclusive of clients with limited English proficiency and persons with legal immigration issues.

Several years later, our newly named program, Mi Gente–VAWA Legal Solutions (a name selected by the staff members, not leadership) and The Translation & Interpreting Center were awarded a $500,000 federal collaboration grant to provide wraparound services for clients.

Innovation—Health Enabling for Listening Professionals (HELP)

In the midst of the 2008 recession, we hosted a discussion about "building upon our strengths" as well as sharing cost-saving strategies. We listened as many of our freelance language subcontractors were reporting symptoms that we recognized as compassion fatigue and vicarious trauma. Three staff members, one with language service expertise and two others with training and trauma expertise, embarked upon a project capitalizing upon their strengths. The collaboration produced our Health Enabling and Listening Professionals (HELP) program.

HELP is a full-day workshop intended to raise awareness about the effects of secondary and vicarious trauma and recapture the helping professional's passion for working with the public. In order to gain recognition and evaluation data, we piloted and refined the program for two years before marketing it for a fee to freelance language and human service professionals.

Participant evaluations spoke of a "refreshing, unexpected, and pleasantly rejuvenating experience." Pre- and post-surveys indicated that HELP workshops increased participants' compassion satisfaction and decreased burnout and secondary traumatic stress. Our HELP workshop became our second earned-income venture for the metropolitan Denver community.

The HELP evaluation data indicated that there is a relationship between the participants' pre-HELP Professional Quality of Life scores and their age, native language, ethnicity, and the length of time that they have worked in the field. That is to say, an individual's age, language, ethnicity, and how long he or she has been a service provider appears to have an influence on the person's compassion satisfaction, burnout, and secondary traumatic stress before completing the workshop. Our finding may have an important implication for direct service providers and suggests an opportunity for supervisors and/or hiring professionals to better understand the factors a listening professional brings to the workplace (age, gender, ethnicity, etc.) that may increase the individual's susceptibility to experiencing vicarious trauma. Perhaps supervisors and/or hiring personnel may wish to increase opportunities to attend to these factors to prevent vicarious trauma. Workshops or trainings such as our

HELP workshop may offset/prevent the development of vicarious trauma symptoms, as evidenced by participants' increased compassion satisfaction scores, and decreased their burnout and secondary trauma scores regardless of their age, language, and ethnicity or how long they have worked in the field. We will continue to build upon this data and explore if future analysis may reveal *which* subscale items have a significant relationship with overall compassion satisfaction, burnout, and secondary trauma stress scores as well as the demographic factors related to each item.

In 2013, The Center for Trauma & Resilience (CTR) conducted 12 HELP workshops for the social services community. To measure the effectiveness of the workshops, HELP participants completed the Professional Quality of Life (ProQoL) measurement instrument, a 30-question self-report survey that measures compassion satisfaction, burnout, and secondary traumatic stress. We had 78 participants complete both a pre-survey and a post-survey.

The ProQoL results revealed a statistically significant decrease ($p < 0.05$) in symptoms of burnout and secondary traumatic stress for HELP participants. The mean score for burnout decreased from 21.60 to 19.68, a low level of burnout. The mean score for secondary traumatic stress decreased from 24.53, an average level, to 20.42, a low level of secondary traumatic stress. The mean score for compassion satisfaction had a mild increase from 40.84 to 41.28, an average level, a relevant but not statistically significant change ($p = 0.35$).

Innovation—Befriending the Body Trauma-Sensitive Yoga

In 2012–2015, our Befriending the Body program was designed, piloted, and evaluated. We adopted the trauma-sensitive model piloted by Bessel Van der Kolk and the Trauma Center at the Justice Resource Institute in Massachusetts.

During our annual BLEAP program-planning session, staff voted to make it a permanent program offering of the agency. Our desire was to provide culturally and linguistically diverse, accessible, and affordable classes to both our clients and the community at large. Initially, we partnered with a local yoga studio; however, the limited demographic and studio limitations quickly became an issue. We quickly surmised that yoga instructors who were people of color or Spanish-speaking were scarce in

Denver. I had a brainstorm: if we can't find them, why not grow them? After securing training funds, 12 new instructors, 10 people of color (nine women), five of whom are Spanish-speaking, received their 200-hour hatha yoga certification.

We promoted our classes to people of color, boys and young men, seniors, monolingual Spanish speakers, Muslims, and plus-sized community members. While services for clients remain without cost, classes for the community have grown into yet another earned-income venture!

We collected evaluations from 151 participants in the Befriending the Body (BTB) trauma-sensitive yoga program. To measure the effectiveness of the series, participants completed pre- and post-evaluations for the Trauma Symptom Checklist (TSC-40) (Table 11.1), Scale of Body Connection (SBC) (Table 11.2), and Quality of Life Enjoyment and Satisfaction Questionnaire (Q-LES-Q-SF) (Table. 11.3) measurement instruments.

And there is more. In late 2015, we joined an initiative to create a more humane environment within the Denver County Jail, launched in 2015, led by Chief Connie Coyle of the Denver Sheriff Department (DSD),

---

TABLE 11.1 ■ **Trauma Symptom Checklist**

The TSC-40 results revealed statistically significant ($p < 0.05$) decreases in the following symptoms:

- Dissociation (raw score decreased from 5.49 to 3.85)
- Anxiety (raw score decreased from 6.71 to 5.27)
- Depression (raw score decreased from 9.05 to 6.43)
- Sexual Abuse Trauma Index (SATI) (raw score decreased from 4.93 to 3.74)
- Sleep Disturbance (raw score decreased from 9.00 to 6.78)
- Sexual Problems (raw score decreased from 5.50 to 4.33)

Note: The TSC-40 is measured on a scale from 0 (never) to 3 (often). Subscale scores are a sum of participant scores for relevant questions.

TABLE 11.2 ■ **Scale of Body Connection**

Scale of Body Connection is a 20-item self-report measure designed to assess body awareness and bodily dissociation in mind-body intervention research. The SBC is measured on a scale from 1 (not at all), 2 (a little bit), 3 (some of the time), 4 (most of the time), to 5 (all of the time), and subscale scores are an average of participant scores.

The SBC results revealed statistically significant ($p < 0.05$) changes:
- Body Awareness (mean score increased from 3.35 to 3.64)
- Body Dissociation (mean score decreased from 2.07 to 1.90)

intended to expand learning opportunities for inmates and create a more humane jail environment. Among the goals were: 1) to reduce recidivism by creating environments that allow for increased reentry and treatment services and 2) to increase opportunities for cross-gendered direct supervision with specialized staff trained in gender and trauma issues.

Acknowledging that 80 percent of the women inmates have victimization histories, we piloted our trauma-sensitive yoga program as part of a larger effort to provide inmates with educational opportunities and prosocial

TABLE 11.3 ■ **Quality of Life Enjoyment and Satisfaction Questionnaire**

Quality of Life Enjoyment and Satisfaction Questionnaire is a self-report measure designed to assess the degree of enjoyment and satisfaction experienced by participants in various areas of daily functioning, including feelings/emotions, physical health/activities, leisure-time activities, health and social relations. Participants indicate degree of enjoyment and satisfaction on a scale of 1 (not at all) to 5 (frequently or all the time), in each of the aforementioned areas.

The Q-LES-Q-SF revealed relevant but not statistically significant changes in overall life satisfaction (mean score increased from 3.73, "fair," to 4.08, "good").

supports so that they are significantly less likely to return to jail or reenter the criminal justice system after release.

Inspiration

We have derived inspiration from everywhere, from *Sesame Street*, to an in-house songstress, to Zumba, the latest dance fitness phenomenon.

Inspiration—Buy What You Sell

In 2005, after watching a *Sesame Street* episode and listening to a National Public Radio announcement about the obesity and diabetes rates for children of color younger than 12 years of age, specifically African Americans and Latinos, I studied the literature on children exposed to violence and trauma and the resulting negative impact on their physical health (Felitti & Anda, 2006). I spoke with the program staff and in an instant, we halted our practice of serving soda, pizza, cookies, puddings, and sugar-laden sweets to children and chose to offer fresher and more nutritious selections. By 2014, we had applied our practice to everyone, adult or child, client/volunteer/guest (including our board members!) attending meetings, groups, or sessions at the agency.

Inspiration—"That Jazz Thing"

In our 14th year and my first as executive director, several staff members said, "Can we discuss hosting a fundraising event that *we would enjoy attending?*" I wasn't surprised. I too had attended each of the ballroom dinners with 100 silent auction items and listened to speaker after speaker attempt to impress the audience by sharing anecdotes of the "good work" being provided by the agency.

Staff members brainstormed and decided to capitalize on the vocal talents of the agency's finance director. It was a departure from the previous 10 years of hosting the "dinner-and-award" prototype fundraiser. Staff created a jazz event, designing everything from the event logo to the jazz-themed silent auction baskets. Our premiere event was underwritten entirely by four people: a local jazz facility manager (friend of the staff), a local natural hair care salon (friend of the director), a small-business proprietor (spouse of a staff member), and a locksmith whose business we helped to launch in 2003 and remains successful to this day.

Our jazz event reigned as our signature event for 10 years, hosting local and international musicians such as Nelson Rangell, Kevin Mahogany, Kim Waters, and Eddie Palmieri and raising more than 10 times our initial investment!

Inspiration—Zumba Fitness Fundraiser

From 2010 to 2012, three staff members became Zumba instructors. Zumba is a trendy, new dance craze and fitness modality that was sweeping the world. Staff members approached management and offered to share their new dance/fitness skills and benefit the fundraising agenda of the agency. We created a weekly summer fundraiser, "Zumba® for a Cause," appealing to and drawing a new and younger demographic of donors via dance fitness.

Inclusiveness

Our founding board members' vision was to "address gaps" and attend to the unserved and underserved populations in our community. The one-size-fits-all, business-as-usual practices shortchanged the vision.

Inclusiveness—Mrs. Mary Washington

I was working one winter evening in 2005 and received a telephone call from a woman who indicated she had "a small amount of money" that she was interested in donating to a nonprofit. She stated that she had several "very specific" requests. She wanted her donation to be awarded to African-American women who were currently or had been victims of intimate partner violence. She wanted assurance that the gift would be given to this demographic, tracked, and reported to her without compromising their confidentiality.

"Can you do that?" she asked.

I replied, "Absolutely!"

Mrs. W. persisted. "Really? I have already contacted several nonprofits in Denver [she listed a few names], and they gave me variations of, 'Sorry we just can't do that,' 'We don't hold funds for a particular group,' and 'We don't, can't, or will not track this kind of demographic data and report to you!'"

I assured Mrs. Washington that we had experience in stewarding memorials for a variety of donors and that I would personally guarantee and supervise every dollar of her (not so small!) anonymous donation. We agreed to meet the following week, and she became, and remains, our *largest* individual donor.

Inclusiveness—Denver Men with Heart

Another signature fundraiser came to fruition after a staff member suggested we explore an avenue to welcome supportive men into our anti-violence/victim assistance movement. As with other ideas, staff and board members leveraged the skills from individuals, in this case men, with whom we were acquainted. Denver Men with Heart asks men to donate their time, labor, and skills to our event. The silent auction donations have ranged from drumming to carpentry, house painting, window washing, lawn care, and floral design. It has been a win–win for all involved. Many of the men who donated owned their businesses, and we highlighted their companies on our website and other social media outlets.

Inclusiveness—Making the Case for Economic Inclusiveness

Our inclusiveness blueprint required that we understand the racial/ethnic makeup of our donors who are people of color and their giving patterns. Our goal was to create a development plan to attract corporate and individual donors of color. We sought to increase donors of color by 10 percent within five years. We implemented a variety of strategies, including the purchase of demographic/cohort-specific donor software; researched the giving patterns of people-of-color–hosted focus groups; expanded the volunteer/board matrix; and redesigned our marketing materials.

Our outcomes: There appeared to be a direct tie between board diversity and fund diversity. We have a more consistently inclusive donor base; secured a major donor of color who remains our largest individual donor; created three earned-income ventures based in inclusiveness; developed more diverse fundraisers; and ultimately, **increased the donors and revenue more than 50 percent** in a five-year period.

And, finally, we purchased our agency home in 2011. We included our clients in the pursuit. Our clients requested a facility in a "home-like" environment, in a neighborhood and on a bus line. They desired to be 10 minutes from a medical facility, a police station, and the district attorney's office. Mission accomplished!

CONCLUSION

I credit staff member morale for positioning the agency to stay fresh and relevant by listening closely to the wishes of our community. An engaged and empowered agency staff offers more "out-of-the-box" thinking and becomes *solution*-focused instead of *problem*-focused—encouraging the agency to thrive. The opportunities for fundraising (in lieu of writing dozens of grant proposals) are limitless. How fabulous is that?!

CHAPTER 12

Back to the Beginning

In *The Mission Myth: Building Nonprofit Momentum Through Better Business* (2012), Maloney concludes:

> *"Mission matters. It's the whole reason you work at your organization. It's why you go through the challenges, face the crises, ask for money, and maneuver many stakeholder relationships, each and every day." (p. 288)*

I stumbled onto the nonprofit path when I began volunteering at a rape crisis center (formally known The Toni Goman Feminist Rape Crisis Center in Columbus, Ohio). I had no idea the path would become a passion, a ministry, a career, and my life's work. And that the 10 years of Sundays (incredible, right?) that I spent with 10 black women—educating ourselves about holistic health and creating strategies to become healthy and stay healthy as we lived and worked in Denver, Colorado—would change my life, morph into workplace policy, and become a critical aspect of trauma work.

In the six years that it took me to write this book, technology has changed radically. In addition, the ethnicity demographic of the metro Denver area is significantly different from 2001, when I became director for The Center for Trauma & Resilience. At that time, metro Denver had an ethnic population of 5 percent African American, 18 percent Latino, 3 percent Asian, 1 percent Native American, and 3 percent multiracial. Currently, the metropolitan Denver population is approximately of 50 percent people of color, the majority of these having Latino origin. However, some things in Denver's trauma-serving nonprofit world have yet to change. My home agency remains one of approximately 30 nonprofit victims' service agencies (along with a few government agencies) in a network called Victim Services Network (VSN) that provide a variety of services from rape crisis to legal assistance for the community. When I began my professional career in Denver, I was one of three people of color employed in a leadership position in the network of service providers. Twenty years later, the network continues to be composed of 30+ nonprofits and the representation of people of color, in general, remains the same! How is this possible? Typically, these are three or four people of color representing nonprofits that serve a specific cultural lens— Latinos, Muslims, or Asian or Native communities. There are few men, and no men of color, who attend regularly.

Solely, by intention and investment, my agency and one other member of the 30 victim-service-network partners, the Victim Assistance Unit (VAU) law enforcement/government agency, *tripled* our capacity with staff of color and men, but the vast majority of VSN organizations have stood still.

In 2014, a federally funded pilot legal service program in Denver made a presentation to my agency. In their third year of operation, the organization described itself as "small and mighty," serving the entire state of Colorado, their mission "to address gaps in legal services" for "the unserved and the underserved." The agency staff was composed of four people—four Caucasian women. At the presentation, they stated that they welcomed referrals from our agency, specifically from Mi Gente, our VAWA Legal Solutions program. Seventy percent of Mi Gente clients are from Latin America and are limited English speakers. When we inquired about the agency's capacity to accept referrals, the director stated, "We have a wonderful—I just can't say enough positive things about her—Spanish-speaking volunteer." Our collective question posed by several CTR staff members was, why wasn't she (or another Spanish-speaking candidate) considered for a paid position?

Our statewide victims services conference—which annually attracts more than 1,200 participants—looks exactly like it did more than 20 years ago. After numerous years of workshops on the value of "diversity and multiculturalism" (several of which I facilitated), less than .05 percent of those in attendance are people of color and they are typically representatives from the same three or four agencies.

As I conclude this book, I can still see that room in Estes Park, Colorado. It is full of executive directors, including the one brave soul who inquired, "Are you serious?" as I presented my budding model on individualized self-care. To which I replied, "Yes, indeed, I am serious."

When executives corner me, asking, "But how can we add one more item to our work?" I reply,

> *"This is the work. We must advocate and practice self-care in concert with inclusiveness/diversity and embrace sustainability in its entirety or risk (and/or remain) being irrelevant and depleting the nonprofit sector of its most valuable resource . . . its people."*

Do I still work more than 40 hours? Sure, it's the nature of the position, but now it is the exception. I balance it by exercising regularly (dance, bike, yoga, weight training), get biweekly massages, eat well, sleep eight hours each night, and revel in my one cup of freshly ground espresso (half-caffeinated) latte! I treasure quality time with family and friends (take lots of mini-vacations). I try to read every night, journal, and pray. As a lifelong learner, even after 12 years, I find ways to stretch my own self-care goals.

References

Bambara, T. C. (1970). On the issue of roles. In *The Black Woman: An Anthology* (pp. 133–135). New York: New American Library.

Bell, H., Kulkarni, S., & Dalton, L. (2003). Organizational prevention of vicarious trauma. *Families in Society: The Journal of Contemporary Human Services*, 84(4), 463–470.

Berceli, D., & Napoli, M. (2006). A proposal for a mindfulness-based trauma prevention program for social workers. *Complementary Health Practice Review*, 11(3), 153–165.

Bober, T., & Regehr, C. (2006). Strategies for reducing secondary or vicarious trauma: Do they work? *Brief Treatment and Crisis Intervention*, 6(1), 1–9. doi:10.1093/brief-treatment/mhj001

Boushey, H., & Glynn, S. J. (2012). There Are Significant Business Costs to Replacing Employees. Washington, DC: Center for American Progress. Retrieved from http://cdn.americanprogress.org/wp-content/uploads/2012/11/CostofTurnover.pdf

Brave Heart, M. Y. H. (2011). *Journal of Psychoactive Drugs*, 43(4), 282–290.

Brave Heart, M. Y. H., & DeBruyn, L. M. (1998). The American Indian holocaust: Healing historical unresolved grief. *American Indian and Alaska Native Mental Health Research*, 8(2), 60–82.

Busch-Armendariz, N., Kalergis, K., & Garza, J. (2009). An Evaluation of the Need for Self-Care Programs in Agencies Serving Adult and Child Victims of Interpersonal Violence in Texas. Institute on Center for Domestic Violence and Sexual Assault Center for Social Work Research. Austin, TX: University of Texas at Austin. Retrieved from www.utexas.edu/ssw/dl/files/cswr/institutes/idvsa/publications/SelfCareReport_090909.pdf

Collins, J. (2001). *Good to Great: Why Some Companies Make the Leap—And Others Don't*. New York: HarperBusiness.

Collins, J. (2005). *Good to Great and the Social Sectors: A Monograph to Accompany Good to Great*. Boulder, CO: Jim Collins.

Crenshaw, K. (1989). Demarginalizing the intersection of race and sex: A black feminist critique of antidiscrimination doctrine, feminist theory and antiracist politics. *U. Chi. Legal F.*, 139–168.

Crenshaw, K. (1991). Mapping the margins: Intersectionality, identity politics, and violence against women of color. *Stanford Law Review*, 43(6), 1241–1299.

Denver District Attorney Victim Services Network. (2001). Vicarious Trauma Guidelines. Retrieved from www.victimservicesnetwork.org/Docs/VT Guidelines_Appendices.doc

Drucker, P. F. (1954). *The Practice of Management*. New York: Harper & Row.

Drucker, P. F. (2005). *Managing Oneself*. Cambridge, MA: Harvard Business Review Press.

Employment Policy Foundation. (2002). Employee turnover—A critical human resource benchmark. *HR Benchmarks*. Washington, DC: Employment Policy Foundation.

Employment Policy Foundation. (2003). Working caregivers show need for workplace flexibility. *The Balancing Act*. Washington, DC: Employment Policy Foundation. Retrieved from https://workfamily.sas.upenn.edu/workplace/employment-policy-foundation

Enright, K. P. (2006). Philanthropy's greatest asset. *Foundation News & Commentary*, 47(4), 44.

Felitti, V. J., & Anda, R. F. (2006). The relationship of adverse childhood experiences to adult medical disease, psychiatric disorders, and sexual behaviors: Implications for healthcare. In Lanius, R., & Vermetten, E.(Eds), *The hidden epidemic: The impact of early life trauma on health and disease* (1-18). Cambridge University Press.

Figley, C. R. (Ed.) (1995). *Compassion Fatigue: Coping with Secondary Traumatic Stress Disorder in Those Who Treat the Traumatized*. New York: Brunner/Mazel.

Grasz, J. (2008). Seventy-eight Percent of Workers Say They Are Burned Out at Work, CareerBuilder.com Survey Finds. Retrieved from www.careerbuilder.com/share/aboutus/pressreleasesdetail.aspx?sd=7/16/2008&id=pr449&ed=12/31/2008

Gutiérrez, K. D., & Rogoff, B. (2003). Cultural ways of learning: Individual traits or repertoires of practice. *Educational Researcher*, 32(5), 19–25. doi:10.3102/0013189X032005019

Herman, J. L. (1992). *Trauma and Recovery*. New York: BasicBooks.

Kawulok, A. (2012). *Denver Center for Crime Victim's Self-Care Program and Organizational Productivity Capstone*. University of Colorado, Denver.

Kleinman, A. (1981). *Patients and Healers in the Context of Culture: An Exploration of the Borderland between Anthropology, Medicine, & Psychiatry*. Berkeley, CA: University of California Press.

Leary, J. D. (2005). *Post Traumatic Slave Syndrome: America's Legacy of Enduring Injury and Healing*. Milwaukie, OR: Uptone Press.

Lipsky, L. van D., & Burk, C. (2009). *Trauma Stewardship: An Everyday Guide to Caring for Self While Caring for Others*. Oakland, CA: Berrett-Koehler Publishers.

Lorde, A. (1998). *A Burst of Light*. Ann Arbor, MI: Firebrand Books.

Maloney, D. (2012). *The Mission Myth: Building Nonprofit Momentum Through Better Business*. San Diego, CA: Business Solutions Press.

McCann, L., & Pearlman, L. A. (1990). Vicarious traumatization: A framework for understanding the psychological effects of working with victims. *Journal of Traumatic Stress*, 3(1), 131–149.

Meichenbaum, D. (2007). *Self-care for Trauma Psychotherapists and Caregivers: Individual, Social, and Organizational Interventions*. Miami, FL: Melissa Institute. Retrieved from http://melissainstitute.org/documents/Meichenbaum_SelfCare_11thconf.pdf

Pearlman, L. A., & Saakvitne, K. W. (1995a). Trauma and the therapist: Countertransference and vicarious traumatization in psychotherapy with incest survivors. In *Compassion Fatigue: Coping with Secondary Traumatic Stress Disorder in Those Who Treat the Traumatized* (pp. 150–177). New York: Norton.

Pearlman, L. A., & Saakvitne, K. W. (1995b). Treating therapists with vicarious traumatization and secondary traumatic stress disorders. In C. R. Figley (Ed.), *Compassion Fatigue: Coping with Secondary Traumatic Stress Disorder in Those Who Treat the Traumatized* (pp. 150–177). New York, NY: Brunner/Mazel, Inc.

Protecting employees, employers and the public: H1N1 and sick leave policies: Hearing before the Committee on Education and Labor. (2009). Washington, DC: U.S. Government Printing Office.

Ratcliffe, J., Wallack, L., Fagnani, F., & Rodwin, V. (1984). Perspectives on prevention: Health promotion vs health protection. In *The End of an Illusion: The Future of Health Policy in Western Industrialized Nations* (pp. 56–84). Berkeley, CA: University of California Press.

Rath, T., & Harter, J. (2010). *Wellbeing: The Five Essential Elements*. New York: Gallup Press.

SAMHSA Center for Mental Health Services. (2005). Addressing Historical Trauma Among African Americans as an HIV Intervention. Retrieved from http://web.archive.org/web/20050505124743/http://mentalhealthaids.samhsa.gov/Spring2005/toolbox1.asp

Stamm, B. H. (Ed.). (1995). *Secondary Traumatic Stress: Self-Care Issues for Clinicians, Researchers, and Educators*. Baltimore, MD: The Sidran Press.

Stevens, S. K. (2001). *Nonprofit Lifecycles: Stage-based Wisdom for Nonprofit Capacity*. Long Lake, MN: Stagewise Enterprises.

The Denver Foundation. (2003). *Inside Inclusiveness: Race, Ethnicity and Nonprofit Organizations*. Denver, CO. Retrieved from www.nonprofitinclusiveness.org/node/54

Tully, M. A. (1999). Lifting our voices: African American cultural responses to trauma and loss. In K. Nader, N. Dubrow, & B. H. Stamm (Eds.), *Honoring Differences: Cultural Issues in the Treatment of Trauma and Loss* (pp. 23–48). Philadelphia, PA: Brunner/Mazel.

van der Kolk, Bessel. (2014). *The Body Keeps the Score: Brain, Mind and Body in the Healing of Trauma*. New York: Viking.

Wasco, S. M., Campbell, R., & Clark, M. (2002). A multiple case study of rape victim advocates' self-care routines: The influence of organizational context 1. *American Journal of Community Psychology*, 30(5), 731–760.

Yount, K.M., DiGirolami, A.M. & Ramakrishnan, U. (2011). Impacts of domestic violence on child growth and nutrition: A conceptual review of the pathways of influence. *Social Science & Medicine, 72*, 1534–1554.

Zinn, H. (1980). *A People's History of the United States*. New York: Harper & Row.

APPENDIX A

The Center for Trauma & Resilience Forms

APPENDIX A-1 ■ New Employee Checklist

Employee's Name: _____ Supervisor's Signature: _____

Executive Director's Initials: _____ Date completed: _____

HUMAN RESOURCES (Initial _____)
_____ Employee Handbook
_____ CTR Benefits Package
_____ Safety Procedures Manual
_____ House Policies & Procedures
_____ Conflict Resolution Policy

PERSONNEL FORMS (Initial _____)
_____ CBI/Background Form
_____ Application/Resume
_____ Employee Master Record
_____ W-4
_____ Personnel Action Notice
_____ I-9 Form and ID
_____ E-Verify
_____ Safety Policy Statement
_____ Work & Family Responsibility Statement
_____ Designated Medical Provider List
_____ Oath of Confidentiality
_____ Health Insurance
_____ Dental Insurance
_____ Vision Insurance
_____ Time Sheet
_____ Telecommuting Request
_____ Leave of Absence Request
_____ CO Mental Health Statute
_____ Non-proselytization Policy
_____ Preventing Sexual Harassment
_____ Elder Abuse Online Training
_____ Employee Payroll Information Form
_____ Employee Deduction Payment Form
_____ Receipt Form: Employee Handbook
_____ Receipt Form: Conflict Resolution
_____ Receipt Form: Benefits Package
_____ Receipt Form: Safety Procedures Manual
_____ Receipt Form: Building Policies
_____ TI Non-Competition Agreement
_____ Emergency Contact Information

Additional Information
_____ Employee Proof of Auto Insurance
_____ Driver's License/Passport
_____ Social Security Card

FUNDRAISING/PUBLIC RELATIONS
(Initial _____)
_____ Agency Development Plan
_____ In-kind Donations
_____ Strategic Plan
_____ Flyer/Mailer Development/Branding

PROGRAM (Initial _____)
_____ Agency Mission Statement
_____ Staff Mission Statement
_____ Inclusiveness Philosophy
_____ Oprah Pay It Forward DVD
_____ Emergency Vouchers
_____ DPD-VAU Orientation
_____ Hotline Orientation
_____ Trauma Recovery Process
_____ Code of Ethics
_____ On-call Response
_____ Monthly Reports
_____ Therapist Interview Questions
_____ Crisis Guidelines Book
_____ Clinical/Program Supervision Schedules
_____ Counselor Meetings
_____ Case/Clinical Review Meetings
_____ DORA Regulatory Application
_____ Victims' Rights Amendment
_____ Job Description
_____ Self-care Plan
_____ Inclusiveness Orientation

PROGRAM VOLUNTEER/OUTREACH
(Initial _____)
_____ Volunteer/Intern Training
_____ Speakers Bureau
_____ Agency Publication Center

APPENDIX A-1 ▪ *(continued)*

ADMINISTRATION (Initial _____)

_____Meet and Greet
_____Telephone In-service
    _____a. Policies
    _____b. Extensions
    _____c. Telephone functions
    _____d. Checking voicemail
_____Agency Keys
_____Business Cards
_____Staff Meetings/Minutes
_____Staff List
_____CTR Website
_____Staff Calendar
_____Introduction to Board
_____Staff Offices
_____Library
_____Supplies
_____Client Files Storage
_____Storage Room
_____Mailboxes
_____In & Out Board
_____Postage Machine
_____Parking
_____Retreats
_____Scrapbooks & Facebook
_____Computer Orientation
    _____a. User ID & Password
_____Committees
    _____a. Retreat
    _____b. Fundraising/Special Events
    _____c. Building
    _____d. Safety
    _____e. Inclusiveness
    _____f. Yoga
    _____g. Blog
_____Administrative Forms
    _____a. Vacation
    _____b. Mileage
    _____c. Purchase Orders
    _____d. Expense Reimbursement
    _____e. Document Circulation

ENVIRONMENTAL (Initial _____)

_____Sanitizing Telephones
_____Building Maintenance
_____Cell Phone Policy
_____Cleaning Schedule
_____Clean Up Common Areas
_____Copier/Fax Machine
_____Recycling
_____Refrigerator/Microwave
_____Scratch Pads/Notepads
_____No Smoking Policy

PROGRAM SPECIFIC ORIENTATON
  (Initial _____)
_____Front Office
_____Hotline
_____Children, Youth and Families
_____Elder
_____Volunteer/Intern
_____HELP/Compassion Fatigue Workshop
_____Befriending the Body Yoga
_____Translation & Interpreting Center
_____Mi Gente - VAWA Legal Solutions

APPENDIX A-2 ■ **Oath of Confidentiality**

I, in the performance of my assigned responsibilities for The Center for Trauma & Resilience, pledge to keep confidential the information obtained about clients, staff, volunteers, or others involved with this agency. This includes information obtained from Denver Police Department offense reports. I will not release client information or identity to anyone except in compliance with the established release of information policy as follows:

Reporting of child abuse and/or neglect as required by the Colorado Children's Code is mandatory. Any knowledge of child abuse and/or neglect must be reported immediately to the appropriate county department or local law enforcement agency, and to supervising staff.

Any knowledge of the danger of imminent harm to a client or others, including but not limited to suicide and homicide, must be reported immediately to the person or persons specifically threatened, appropriate law enforcement, and supervisory staff.

Mandatory reports of abuse and exploitation of at-risk elders: A specified person who observes the abuse or exploitation of an at-risk elder (any person who is seventy years of age or older) who has reasonable cause to believe that an at-risk elder has been abused or has been exploited or is at imminent risk of abuse or exploitation must file a report.

Client information may be released to those persons having direct need for such information to provide a continuity of client care. Client permission must be obtained prior to the information being released outside of this agency.

Within these guidelines, if there is any breach in confidentiality or client anonymity, I may be terminated immediately and could be held personally liable.

Name (Print) _____

Signature _____ Date _____

APPENDIX A-3 ■ **Presentation of Self-Assessment Guidelines**

Please complete the answers to these questions in essay form.

- Identify those areas where you are satisfied with your POS as it now exists.
- Also, identify those areas where you feel you want or need to improve.
- Please use examples of your behavior to demonstrate your answers.
- Feel free to share this assignment with significant people who may be in a position to observe you. Please include people who are not considered to be "friends" and would offer you an objective assessment.

PRESENTATION OF SELF – ASSESSMENT QUESTIONS

Presentation of Self (Symbolic)

1. What are my symbols? And what do they say about me? What is my style?
2. What are other people picking up from my symbols?
3. Are my symbols saying what I want them to say?
4. Are any of my symbols/style getting in the way of my achieving personal or professional goals?
5. Are they presenting a challenge to a community (or group) to whom I would like to belong?

Presentation of Self (Nonverbal)

1. What does my physical bearing say about me?
2. How can I get more feedback about my body language? Who is in a position to observe me and provide me with honest feedback?
3. Who do I know that exhibits "good" body language? What does he/she do that is "good"? Do I present myself as well as this person? What can I learn from this person?

Presentation of Self (Verbal)

1. How is my speech? Do I talk too fast or too slow? How is my rhythm?
2. How is my grammar?
3. How are my sending skills? Are people receiving my messages?
4. How are my thoughts presented? Am I organized? Disorganized? Tangential?
5. Could I be accused of verbal overkill or under-kill?
6. Do I ask for feedback? Do I use it when it is given? Why or why not?

(Continued)

APPENDIX A-3 ■ *(continued)*

Presentation of Self (General)

1. Maturity — Would I be considered by someone observing me as mature or immature?
2. Poise — Do I have poise or do I lack it? Do I have it under certain conditions?
3. Assertiveness — Am I appropriately assertive? Passive? Aggressive?
4. Warmth — Am I considered warm? Aloof? Cold? Cordial? Friendly?
5. Leadership — Am I considered a leader? By whom? What leadership behaviors do I evidence? Or am I considered a follower? A team player?
6. Humor — Do I inject humor into situations appropriately? Do I offend others with my humor or my humorlessness?

© 2016 The Center for Trauma & Resilience

APPENDIX A-4 ■ Safety Policy Statement

To: All CTR Employees

It is the intent of The Center for Trauma & Resilience (CTR) to provide the safest possible working conditions for employees.

It is our intention that no employee should perform any task that he or she believes is unsafe. All employees will be responsible for their performance and adherence to safety rules. It is each employee's responsibility to correct/report unsafe conditions immediately.

CTR recognizes their responsibility to provide a safe, health-promoting work environment, to abide by all applicable regulations, to communicate our commitment to safety, to correct unsafe conditions in an expedient manner, and to require unqualified commitment from each employee.

Executive Director's Signature: _____

Date: _____

© 2016 The Center for Trauma & Resilience

APPENDIX A-5 ■ **Conflict Resolution Guidelines**

A. COMMUNICATION AT THE CENTER

1. Directly offer constructive feedback.
2. Share relevant information and try new ideas.
3. Be accountable for your wants, needs, and boundaries in the workplace.
4. Actively listen to other's opinions considering both facts and feelings.
5. Be courteous and cooperative.
6. Actively participate in retreats, meetings, and discussions by giving feedback when asked without fear of reprisal.
7. Be accountable for your participation in the conflict resolution process.

B. SUGGESTIONS FOR CONFLICT RESOLUTION

1. These guidelines do not supersede the Center's policies and procedures.
2. When dealing with conflict resolution:

   C larify   **A** cknowledge   **V** erify   **E** mpathize   **S** ummarize
3. Be assertive and direct. Go to the person with whom you are in conflict. Deal with conflict in calm, open, and immediate (if possible) fashion.
4. While meeting with the person with whom you are in conflict, share information and feelings to gain knowledge.
5. If the issue cannot be resolved, agree to disagree or ask for help from a person willing to serve as a mediator.
6. If you find you are a third party to a conflict:
   a. Redirect the person (first party) back to the person with whom he or she has the conflict (second party).
   b. When the third party is concerned that conflict issues remain unresolved, the third party should attempt to act as an informal mediator between the persons in conflict. Information must be shared within the threesome, but should not go beyond.
   c. ALL PARTIES—STOP HERE! Do not go to a fourth party. If necessary, encourage the persons in conflict to use formal mediation or grievance procedures as detailed in personnel policies.

Acknowledgment of Receipt

I have received a copy of the *Conflict Resolution Guidelines*. I understand that I am to become familiar with its contents. Upon signing this acknowledgment of receipt, I agree to participate in the conflict resolution process as outlined.

Employee Signature _____ Date _____

APPENDIX A-6 ▪ Vacation Leave and Donor Form

Date: _____

DONOR:
Employee's Name: _____

RECIPIENT:
Employee's Name: _____

Donor's Available Hours of Leave as of the date of this request: _____

Effective Date of Donation:

I, _____, freely donate _____ hours of my available vacation hours listed above to _____. I understand that I am waiving the rights to these hours and once donated they are no longer available for my use. I also understand that should I deplete my vacation leave, I will be unable to receive the hours I have donated. The Center for Trauma & Resilience has my permission to decrease my available vacation leave by the designated number of donated hours. I am fully aware that this is an irrevocable agreement and cannot be reversed at any time, for any reason.

Signed: _____ Date: _____
　　　　　　　　Donating Employee's Signature

Signed: _____ Date: _____
　　　　　　　　Executive Director's Signature

© 2016 The Center for Trauma & Resilience

APPENDIX A-7 ■ **Case Presentation Outline**

Date _____ Presenter _____

I. CASE AND CLIENT INFORMATION:

   a. Client's name (and age, ethnicity, and other pertinent description)

     _____

     _____

     _____

   b. How was client referred to Hotline? _____

   c. Type of trauma/victimization _____

   d. Reason for presenting the case (legal liability, high-profile crime, high risk, community issues, mental health issues, unusual situations, professional struggle, or success story)

     _____

     _____

     _____

     _____

   e. Brief chronological narrative of crime (who's involved, what occurred, when it occurred, trauma signs, client needs, and CTR response)

     _____

     _____

     _____

     _____

   f. CTR response has been complicated by (optional)

     _____

     _____

     _____

     _____

(Continued)

II.   CASE MANAGEMENT ISSUES:

What is the question that you believe will either advance your knowledge or the knowledge of your peers regarding the case presentation?

_____

_____

_____

What do you want your peers to learn from this case?

_____

_____

_____

Counselor's plan for the case (if appropriate)

_____

_____

_____

Case Management response/follow-up

_____

_____

_____

III. CASE PRESENTATION UPDATE (Review case and pertinent issues):
Client's response to case management suggestions

_____

_____

_____

APPENDIX A-8 ■ Quality Assurance Guidelines

Criteria for case review have been established to ensure quality of service to clients. Case records are one way to reflect what services were provided and how they were provided. Staff must adhere to 80% compliance for Quality Assurance (QA).

All cases will be reviewed for:

1. **Safety and Security Issues.** All clients will be screened for physical safety and that they are in a nonhazardous environment. Using available information while working the case, it needs to be established to the best of our ability if clients may be harmed or may harm themselves or others. Appropriate actions must be taken to report information to the proper authorities and/or agency.

2. **Support: Emotional and Physical Assistance.** This is a service that is always offered by CTR: checking for the client's personal support systems, offering CTR counseling (using the CTR screening criteria in the process), and/or providing counseling referrals. In cases that are appropriate, offering Specialist support, Senior Companion services, etc. are also offered.

3. **Legal Issues.** All cases should ascertain and explore areas related to: confidentiality; verbal permission to disclose case information; screening for and reporting neglect or abuse as required by law; screening for and reporting any imminent harm to self or others. In cases where written information is requested, a Release of Information form should be completed by the client. When there is client contact via an in-house/home visit session, the Agency Disclosure form must be signed and attached to the case.

4. **Plan of Action.** All cases should outline the issues to be addressed and clearly demonstrate the direction of the case and future service plan.

5. **Referrals and Services Offered.** All referrals and services offered must be documented in the case file. (This includes when services/referrals are offered and the client declines.)

6. **Completeness.** All client cases must be coherent with the case plan.

7. **Case must be filed appropriately.** All cases must be filed in the Open or Closed files or have a case sign-out form.

APPENDIX A-9 ■ Suggestions for Choosing a Therapist

Once you have decided to start therapy, choosing a therapist can be an intimidating process. Doing some preparation can help you be successful. The following suggestions can help you accomplish your goals:

1. **Call** and/or visit with several therapists before making your decision about which therapist you want to see. Your relationship with your therapist is an important aspect of what makes counseling work. You will want to ask the therapists:

   What model or type of counseling they provide

   How long they have been in practice

   Ask about their formal education. Degrees? Licenses?

   What is their specialty?

   How long do they anticipate working with you?

2. **Make a list** of what you want to accomplish in therapy. Briefly discuss what you hope to accomplish and ask them if they think they can help you reach your goals. Writing it down doesn't mean that you will accomplish it, but it will give the therapist, and you, a better understanding of what you are looking for in therapy and may help you discover some of your long-term goals.

3. **Listen** to what they say, and just as importantly, how they say it. Do the therapists put you at ease? Are their speech pattern, accent, and vocabulary easy for you to follow and understand? Do they sound empathetic and caring?

4. **Trust yourself** and your impressions. If one therapist looks more impressive on paper, but another one makes you feel more comfortable, go with your heart and pick the one whom you feel you can be more honest with. Research has shown that the relationship between the therapist and client is the single greatest element in the facilitation of positive change and growth for the client.

APPENDIX A-9 ■ *(continued)*

The Center for Trauma & Resilience suggests the following considerations to help you choose a therapist:

A. **Cost.** Will the therapist give you a free first consultation? What types of payment are accepted? Does the therapist accept Victim's Compensation, Medicaid, or private insurance? Does the therapist offer a sliding scale based on your ability to pay? Does the therapist accept pro bono clients? Does the therapist accept Victim's Compensation as full payment for services rendered?

B. **Location.** Is the therapist's office accessible? Does the location create a hardship for you?

C. **Gender, Ethnicity, Culture, and Language.**

   Would you feel more comfortable working with a man or a woman?

   Do you prefer to work with a person of a particular ethnicity?

   What age?

   Do you have any specific communication needs due to language or ability?

   Do you have other preferences for a therapist?

D. **Availability.**

   Does the therapist have emergency coverage services?

   Are telephone crisis sessions available?

   Is the therapist available to talk with partners, family, friends, etc.?

E. **Assessment and Evaluation.**

   Can the therapist provide assessments or evaluations if needed?

   Does the therapist work with providers who could assist with medication if needed?

APPENDIX B

Sample Self-Care Forms

APPENDIX B-1 ■ Developing Your Self-Care Plan

COMPONENTS OF A SELF-CARE PLAN
Physical
Emotional
Financial
Intellectual
Spiritual

EXAMPLES:

Physical
What do I want to accomplish?
  Learn to swim

How am I going to accomplish this?
  Take swimming lessons

How will my progress be measured?
  Demonstrated evidence of swimming lessons

What will be different? (Measurable)
  I will be able to swim across the length of a pool and back.

Additional Benefits:
  Physical exercise
    Lose weight
    Reduce blood pressure
    Decrease anxiety symptoms
    Decrease depression symptoms
    Decrease medication
  Relaxation
  Increase social support

Emotional
What do I want to accomplish?
  Better communication with my partner

How am I going to accomplish this?
  Spend more quality time together

How will my progress be measured?
  Set dates with set plans

What will be different? (Measurable)
  12 dates (one per month)
  I plan 6 dates, he/she plans 6 dates

Additional Benefits:
  See and do new things
  Develop new interests and skills
  Relaxation

Financial
What do I want to accomplish?
  Save money

WHAT DOES A SELF-CARE PLAN LOOK LIKE?

Ask yourself:
What do I want to accomplish?
How am I going to accomplish this?
How will my progress be measured?
What will be different?

How am I going to accomplish this?
  Open a savings account
  Stop buying coffee on my way to work
  Deposit $20 each paycheck

How will my progress be measured?
  Savings account entries

What will be different? (Measurable)
  I will have saved $480.00 by the end of the year

Additional benefits:
  Establish emergency fund
  Go on a trip
  Increase financial independence
  Make a purchase

Intellectual
What do I want to accomplish?
  Learn about edible mushrooms in Colorado

How am I going to accomplish this?
  Research: read books, journals, and magazines, and ask for recommendations from friends, experts, or librarians

How will my progress be measured?
  Purchase or library check-out of books, internet articles, class attendance

What will be different? (Measurable)
  By reading one article each month, I will know more about edible Colorado mushrooms and feel more confident when picking and eating mushrooms.

Additional benefits:
  Relaxation
  Meeting others interested in mushrooms would increase social support.
  Stimulate both the right and left side of the brain
  Exercise
  Enjoy the outdoors

APPENDIX B-1 ■ *(continued)*

NOW IT'S YOUR TURN:

Spiritual
What do I want to accomplish?

How am I going to accomplish this?

How will my progress be measured?

What will be different? (Measurable)

Decide how and when you will enact your plan.

How will you know it is working and what will be different?

You can get support to accomplish your goals from:
- Self-care buddy
- Rewards and milestones
- Creativity

APPENDIX B-2 ■ Self-Care Progress Report

	Physical	Emotional	Financial	Intellectual	Spiritual
Goal					
Measurement					
What will be different?					
January					
February					
March					
April					
May					
June					
July					
August					
September					
October					
November					
December					
PROGRESS	At % of goal	At % of goal	At % of goal	At % goal	At % of goal

APPENDIX B-3 ■ Self-Care Goal Examples

Physical
- Lose/Gain weight
- Address an ongoing medical/acute issue
- Join Weight Watchers
- Join a bike club
- Get a recreation center card
- Learn to ski/swim/snowboard
- Lower my BMI
- Get pregnant
- Join a bowling club
- Run a half marathon/walk a 5K
- Take a yoga/Pilates class
- Take 12 Hot Yoga sculpt-with-weight classes
- Join a fitness club
- Join Curves
- Get a personal trainer
- Stop smoking
- Take Taekwondo
- Climb a fourteener
- Stop drinking soda
- Lower blood pressure/cholesterol
- Get Lasik surgery
- Complete a triathlon
- Lower blood cholesterol
- Learn to belly dance/salsa/cumbia
- Give up milk chocolate for dark chocolate
- Get braces
- Go to a sleep clinic
- Get quarterly facials

Emotional
- Explore a fear or phobia
- Detox from energy-negative friendships—end the friendships by sending letters
- Create a will, custody/guardianship
- Set limits with in-laws (only two holidays per year)
- Schedule monthly date night (that doesn't involve food or movies)
- Begin a genogram
- Write a letter to parents explaining some position
- Begin therapy/End therapy
- Take a mini vacation each quarter
- Change one thing about my style
- Get married/divorced
- Ask a woman/man out
- Stop drinking alcohol for a year
- Attend AA/Alanon meetings
- Take monthly 1:1 outings with sons/daughters
- Get an elective surgery
- Join a dating service
- Restore and frame old family photos or prints
- Get my DNA and trace my roots
- Go on a vacation alone
- Adopt a rescue animal
- Vacation with family, friends, or partner
- Explore the adoption option
- Clean out my closet and get rid of things I have not worn in 2 years
- Resign from a board/club/group/ anything that bores me
- Begin a year of No to any new requests for my time

Financial
- Buy a new outfit once a month
- Give up Starbucks for a year—buy an airline ticket
- Spend $500 on a Pay It Forward project
- Take a budgeting class
- Save money (various amounts)
- Raise my credit score to 750
- Buy a car with cash

(Continued)

APPENDIX B-3 ■ *(continued)*

- Get a financial advisor
- Buy/Sell a house
- Pay off credit card
- Buy expensive cookware
- Select a charity to volunteer or to donate
- Create a college fund
- Get my passport and travel out of the country
- Begin or join an investment club
- Get a part-time job
- Buy a savings bond or IRA
- Give up chips/red meat/soda/coffee, etc.

Intellectual
- Begin graduate school
- Finish writing my book
- Take the LCSW/LPC exam
- Delete Facebook account
- Go skydiving/white-water rafting
- Become a Zumba instructor
- Get my art therapy certificate
- Take a cake decorating class
- Attend 5 restaurant tours
- Visit 7 art galleries
- Paint a picture
- Read 4 Shakespeare plays
- Read 10 books from the New York Times Best Seller list
- Start a book club
- Present at a national conference
- Write a paper/a series of poems/short stories/a journal article
- See 12 foreign films
- Begin to learn a language other than English
- Learn a new skill/single parenting/conflict management
- Take piano/guitar/voice lessons

- Audition for a play
- Take an improv class
- Read 6 Latino authors
- Travel to a foreign country
- Write a book for children
- Learn a new Microsoft software application
- Organize a boycott
- Get a tutor
- Create a recycling program
- Visit local art museum(s) 12 times

Spiritual
- Try yoga or meditation
- Visit various religious organizations
- Get a tattoo with my daughter
- Host quarterly dinner parties
- Begin an urban garden
- Visit a mosque
- Stop/Start going to church
- Go on camping/hiking trips
- Join a choir
- Join a writers' group
- Go off the grid—no spouse, kids, computers, or cell phone for a weekend
- Learn to play the conga drum/another musical instrument
- Scrapbook quarterly with friends
- Clean house top to bottom and host a garage sale
- Find a new volunteer opportunity
- Legally change my name
- Locate my birth parents
- Become a vegetarian/vegan
- Go on a silent retreat for 3 to 10 days
- Get monthly massages for a year
- Become a tutor for kids that have trouble reading

APPENDIX B-4 ■ Kathi Fanning's 2012 — 100 "Things To Do" List

Hike at Devil's Backbone

Hike at Bobcat Ridge

Early morning walk at Boyd Lake with the dogs

Take the dogs to the dog park

Bird-watching tour

Tent camping

Bowling

Outdoor concert at Foote Lagoon

Outdoor concert at Chapunga

Bike ride to the faces bridge

Riding my bike to the library

Planting a garden

Madi and Mom night out

Going to dinner and a movie with Alex

Golfing

Playing laser tag

Professional manicure

Professional pedicure

Massage

Going to an Eagles game

Girlfriend trip

Going to a Colorado Ice game

Going to a Rockies game

Making a fondue dinner

Hiking in Rocky Mountain National Park

Ghost-hunting expedition

Visiting a new place in Colorado

Travel out of state

Taking a haunted tour

Making a mosaic

Scrapbooking my 100 things to do that make me happy

Working on a project with my dad

Going to a museum opening

Going dancing

Meeting with an old friend for dinner and catching up

Going out to coffee with a friend

Having a martini with friends

Playing poker with friends

Going on a picnic

Going fishing

Wading at Glenhaven

Riding in a motor boat

Paddling a canoe or kayak

Going to church on Easter Sunday then hiding eggs

Singing songs at the piano with my mom and sister

Going to lunch and shopping with my sister

Learning how to do a new craft or art project (9 quilts and counting)

Walking through downtown Estes Park

Swimming in an outdoor pool

Soaking in natural hotsprings

Road trip

Drive around and look at Christmas lights

Visiting out-of-town friends or family

Game night with friends

Getting together with a college roommate

Going on a hike to the stone house

Having ice cream at Dairy Delight

Going to a show at the Rialto

Going to a show at the Lincoln theatre in Cheyenne

Going fossil hunting

Decorate for Christmas

Make sushi with Ruthie via Skype

Night hike

Visit Benson Park

Visit Viestenz-Smith Park

Going to the mountains to look for moose

Watching a fireworks show

Visiting the mountains to see the leaves change

Sit out on my patio and drink tea and do puzzles

Hot tub soak

Outdoor patio happy hour

Have a pajama day

Sleep on really soft sheets

Watch a really scary movie

Visit a historical site

Totally surprise someone with a great present

Pick pumpkins

Get rid of my old computer and buy a new one

Find pants that are long enough hopefully on sale

Go to a CSU game

Pay off a credit card

Redecorate the living room

Redecorate the bathroom

Finish a jigsaw puzzle

Visit a water park

Take my nieces out

Go to a wedding and stay through the reception only if it's fun

Make another JibJab card

Celebrating Alex's graduation with a party

Movie quality romantic evening– pictures not available

Sitting around in the condo at Keystone

Visit a winery

Go for a walk at North Lake Park in the fall

Get my wedding ring fixed

Watch a parade

Blowing something up with fireworks

Attend a book club meeting

Make a list of 25 new things I would like to try

Swimming in a lake or ocean

Other Forms

APPENDIX C-1 ■ **Staff Mission Statement**

"To create and maintain a cooperative work environment which promotes accountability, trust, and respect for individual strengths and team growth, while sharing a commitment to a common vision."

November 4, 1992

APPENDIX C-2 ■ **Inclusiveness Philosophy**

The Center for Trauma & Resilience is an inclusive agency that values the contributions and cultures of all its stakeholders and clients. We create an organizational culture based on respect, accountability, and trust. Our commitment to inclusiveness is evidenced by our agency's policies, practices, and strategic plans.

APPENDIX C-3 ■ **Inclusiveness Activity Examples**

THE EXPANDING NONPROFIT INCLUSIVENESS EXAMPLES OF
STAFF-SELECTED QUARTERLY TRAININGS

The agency inclusiveness efforts include quarterly trainings, discussions, presentations, and visits to local exhibits. Activities are based on staff interest, whether they
are contemporary or historical. Quarterly events may have a yearlong theme or they
may be spontaneous, inspired by current events. All activities and discussions are
aimed at increasing knowledge, cultural responsiveness, and social justice.

We have incorporated two inclusiveness trainings into our annual staff calendar
which are facilitated by local experts and consultants:

1. Anti-racism and micro-aggressions trainings (for example, The Four "I's" of
   Oppression: Ideological, Institutional, Interpersonal, Internalized)
2. Ethical communication training

Examples of other quarterly events include:
Museum and Gallery Tours
- Black American West Museum & Heritage Center
- Chicano Humanities and Arts Council (CHAC) Gallery and Cultural Center
- Denver Buddhist Temple
- Design for the Other 90% at the Redline
- It's All About Relating – It's About China, Wang Gongxin's Exhibition
  at the Redline
- RACE: Are We So Different? History Colorado Center
- Stiles African American Heritage Center
- Tribal Paths: Colorado's American Indians 1500 to Today,
  History Colorado Center

Community and National Events
- Biennial of the Americas – Poverty Roundtable
- The Democratic National Convention (2008), Denver, CO
- The Latino Summit — Auraria campus, Denver, CO
- *Ma Rainey's Black Bottom* by August Wilson, at The Shadow Theater
  Company

Lectures
- *American Indian Boarding School Experience – a Navajo Perspective*
  presented by Bessie Smith
- *Estara Health and Wellness: Curanderismo – Sound Healing, Aromatherapy
  and Auricular Therapy* presented by Sofia Chavez

(Continued)

- *History of Ramadan* presented by Abdalla Khalifa
- *The Israel and Palestinian Peace Initiatives* presented by Mohamed Jodeh, The Colorado Muslim Society and Seeking Common Grounds
- *The New Jim Crow: Mass Incarceration in the Age of Colorblindness* presented by Michelle Alexander
- *Spoken Word Poetry* presented by Dominique Christina Johnson
- *Transracial Adoptions* presented by Susan Devan Harness
- *Violence in the LGBTQ Community* presented by The Center — Advancing LGBT Colorado

Film, Book, and Article Discussions
- *Babel* (film)
- *Bowling for Columbine* (film)
- "Color Blind or Just Plain Blind: The Pernicious Nature of Contemporary Racism," by John Dovidio and Samuel Gaertner (article)
- *Crash* (film)
- *Fire*; *Earth*; *Water* (Deepa Mehta's trilogy of films)
- *In the Time of the Butterflies* by Julie Alvarez (film)
- *Paradise Now* (film)
- *Rabbit-Proof Fence* (film)
- "Sisters of the 'Yogic' Yam: bell hooks and the Yoga in Self-Recovery" by Sariane Leigh (article)
- *Traces of the Trade: A Story from the Deep North* (film)

Staff Discussions
- Diversity fatigue
- Family genograms
- Making the case for economic inclusiveness
- Trayvon Martin, his life, his death, and the George Zimmerman trial verdict

APPENDIX C-4 ■ BLEAP (Bettering the Lives of Employees and Agency Programs)

Staff Benefits

___ $200 Training Budget
(per staff member)

___ Per Diem for Travel (increase)

___ 20–30 minutes Meditation Break
(daily/ once a week)

___ Bonus during the Holidays

___ Self-Care Quarterly Bonus

___ Staff Board Game Day Retreat

___ Staff Overnight Retreat

Building

___ New Conference Tables and Chairs
(donate)

___ TI Center Furniture

___ Artwork for halls

___ Meditation Cushions and Yoga Balls

___ New Desks/Standing Desks

___ Coffee/Espresso Machine for 3rd floor

___ Flat-screen TVs/Blu-ray or DVD

___ Smart Phones for Hotline Staff

___ Copy Machine for the 3rd floor

___ Replace Hardwood Floors
on the 3rd floor

___ New Roof

___ New Wheelchair Ramp

___ Security System/Intercom

___ Landscape

___ Back Door with Awning

Office Furniture/Supplies

___ Yoga Supplies
(bolsters, straps, and back jacks)

___ New Front Office Furniture

___ New 3rd Floor Copier

___ New Blinds for Front Office and
Conference Rooms

___ New Photo Camera (Nikon or Canon)

___ Video Software (create movies/videos)

___ T-shirts (organization)

Fundraising/PR

___ Staff Pitch Party

___ Zumba for a Cause
(yearlong space location)

___ Yoga Conference

___ Women's Retreat (quarterly)

___ Food Flicks Recipe Book

___ Trauma Yoga/ Teacher Training
Workshop

___ Signature Event

___ Spanish Classes

___ Consulting

___ Expand HELP Workshop

___ PR Firm

Program/Services

___ Magdalena Chrysalis Award

___ Yoga Studio/Zumba Studio

___ ESL Classes for Clients

___ Social Enterprise Consulting

___ National Training for Yoga Students

___ Food Flicks Nutrition Expansion
Classes

___ Trauma Art Therapy

___ Service Day

___ Book Club for Clients

___ Researcher and Evaluator

APPENDIX C-5 ■ **Potluck Sign-up**

POTLUCK OCCASION

_____

DATE & TIME

_____

APPETIZER	SALAD
_____	_____
_____	_____

ENTREE	VEGGIE ENTREE
_____	_____
_____	_____

VEGETABLE	DRINKS
_____	_____
_____	_____

DESSERT	FRUIT
_____	_____
_____	_____

CLEAN-UP
_____ Everyone on Staff _____

CPSIA information can be obtained
at www.ICGtesting.com
Printed in the USA
BVHW061139300620
582537BV00005B/329